ENDORSEMENTS

For decades now Bishop Joseph Mattera has been a voice of reason and motivation for the Body of Christ. He has an uncanny ability to provide clarity and direction towards emerging trends coupled with keen discernment that allows him to write the proper prescription for what ails us. He has done it again with *The Purpose, Power, and Process of Prophetic Ministry*. This pro-prophetic treatise is one of the most balanced and ecclesiologically sound descriptions of the prophetic I have ever read!

Dr. Kyle Searcy
Senior Pastor, Fresh Anointing Church
Montgomery, AL

This book is a must read for every member of the Body of Christ, particularly those who sense any calling into prophetic ministry. Bishop Mattera masterfully communicates the role and importance of the entire five-fold ministry (APEST) and how the prophet's ministry is to be inter-woven to display the fulness of the ministry of Jesus. With all the recent controversy concerning inaccurate prophetic declarations, the need for introspection and balance is brought to the forefront so that adjustments can be made to prevent past mistakes from being repeated. Bishop Mattera lovingly reveals the purpose of the prophetic ministry within the Church and how it is designed to build up the Body of Christ and not be the source of confusion and controversy.

Pastor Robert Gay
High Praise Worship Center

Dr. Joseph Mattera is held in the highest regard around the world and is loved, honored, and respected by all who know him and has now created a timeless and timely gift to the Body of Christ around the world. *The Purpose, Power, and Process of Prophetic Ministry* is biblically sound and filled with historical truth. This masterfully written book will in no doubt become the "go to" resource for understanding the gift of prophecy as it relates and functions in our lives today. No stone left unturned, no question left unanswered, this is Joseph at his best, delivering reason, resolve, and resolution to the world of the prophetic we find ourselves so consumed with today.

Ward Simpson
President, GOD TV

Joseph Mattera is a great friend, advocate, and practitioner of prophetic function; this makes him an important voice to the prophetic movement at large. He is also a true teaching apostle in the church whose track record in ministry undergirds his ability to communicate the biblical truths regarding the prophetic in a way that can be embraced and implemented at the coalface level of ministry expression.

Enjoy this book, work through it slowly and make sure that you recommend it to all your brothers and sisters in Christ who are aspirational about seeing the prophetic ministry mature to a place of activation in the saints in such a way that Christ is glorified!

David Balestri
Executive Consultant of Elite Human Development

Joseph Mattera's, *The Purpose, Power, and Process of Prophetic Ministry*, is a comprehensive analysis of the prophetic movements around the world. The insight into the impact of eschatology upon culture was very insightful, with which I would agree. I deeply appreciated the focus on Jesus and the early apostles' servant-leadership model. This book is a goldmine of information relating to what is happening in the church today. The insights regarding the Kingdom to come, and the Kingdom now, were very important. Joseph points out where there are problems and where there are signs of hope for the churches and the Kingdom of God. This is a book anyone who wants to be better appraised on the apostolic /prophetic movement should have in their personal library.

Randy Clark
Overseer of the Apostolic Network of Global Awakening
President of Global Awakening Theological Seminary

Bishop Joseph Mattera addresses some very important topics and issues regarding the prophetic in *The Purpose, Power, and Process of Prophetic Ministry*. I appreciate the fact that he does not come from an antagonistic or anti the gifts approach, but as one who himself has interfaced with and operated in the prophetic. Yet, as one who is a deep processor and theological thinker, he delves into some important aspects.

Personally, I've often said that the ability to give prophetic words or words of knowledge, does not necessarily mean one is operating in the office of the fivefold ministry gift of prophet as referred to in Ephesians 4:11-12. These are not to be used as authoritative titles, but rather more to describe function to equip and prepare God's people for personal growth and service, and to build up the Body of Christ.

The equipping gifts, including office of prophet are important functions in the church, and no doubt we definitely have a need for those who have prophetic insight today.

A.W. Tozer, in "The Gift of Prophetic Insight", says it well when he wrote about the importance of understanding present conditions:

> *Today we need prophetic preachers; not preachers of prophecy merely, but preachers with a gift of prophecy...We need the gift of discernment again in our pulpits. It is not ability to predict that we need, but the anointed eye, the power of spiritual penetration and interpretation, the ability to appraise the religious scene as viewed from God's position, and to tell us what is actually going on.*

Take the time to read, pray through, and study as you go through this book by Joseph Mattera. May it provoke you to go deeper in personal consecration and higher in expectation in the Lord, while contending for the authentic.

Doug Stringer
Founder and President of Somebody Cares

Drawing from his decades of experience and from recent controversies related to prophets and prophecy, Joseph Mattera gives us solid ground upon which to stand as charismatic and Pentecostal people seek the presence of the Lord Jesus Christ. While addressing numerous issues that have historically, and presently, impacted Spirit-filled congregations, he carefully balances the Apostle Paul's guidance that we "desire spiritual gifts, but especially that you may prophesy," with the knowledge that "we know in part and we prophesy in part" (1 Corinthians 14:1; 13:9). Based firmly on Scripture, this is a must-read book.

Dr. Doug Beacham
General Superintendent
International Pentecostal Holiness Church

THE PURPOSE, POWER, AND PROCESS OF PROPHETIC MINISTRY

DR. JOSEPH MATTERA

eGenCo

Publisher—eGenCo

eGenCo
Chambersburg, Pennsylvania

Email: info@egen.co
Website: www.egen.co

facebook.com/egenbooks

youtube.com/egenpub

pinterest.com/eGenDMP

instagram.com/egen.co

Library of Congress Cataloging-in-Publication Data

Library of Congress Control Number: 2021907882

ISBN: 978-1-68019-022-9   Paperback
          978-1-68019-023-6   eBook

TABLE OF CONTENTS

FOREWORD

As I write these words on January 23, 2021, I can honestly say that I have never seen a moment of such deep spiritual deception within the Church in my forty-nine years in the Lord; in particular, the deception within the charismatic wing of the Church, to which I belong. It is not merely a matter of many believers looking to Donald Trump in an unhealthy and idolatrous way, as if he was some political messiah. It is not just the wild and crazy QAnon conspiracy theories that many believers have embraced, holding to them almost as if they were sacred gospel truths. Chiefly, it is the fact that a large chorus of prophets predicted that Trump would be reelected, guaranteeing his victory even after Joe Biden had been certified by Congress.

Some continued to guarantee Trump's victory even after Biden's inauguration, while others claimed that Trump was the true president in God's sight. They believed that Biden would soon be removed. Worse still, some of these "prophets" issued threats against those who would dare challenge them or call them to account. They claimed to speak for God as they did so, saying things like, "I the Lord say to you, 'Do not touch…My prophets!'"[1] This is spiritual manipulation and prophetic deception at the highest level, and millions of believers have been negatively impacted in the process. Who will be there to pick up the pieces of all those believers whose faith is now shattered? Who will be there to help clean up this mess that has brought so much reproach to the name of the Lord?

The story of the failed Trump prophecies has become a significant subject in the secular media. One young man posted online that he had been telling his family, none of whom were believers, that Trump would be reelected based on the words of the prophets. He thought it would glorify the Lord

1   Ps. 105:15

when Trump was miraculously inaugurated. Now, he said, he doesn't believe he can ever talk to his family about the Lord again.

A colleague of mine sent this to me after a pastor he knew posted it online:

> *The smoke is beginning to clear away and once again the church has a mess on its hands—especially in evangelical Christianity. It saddens me to think of the thousands now walking away from their faith—disillusioned and blaming so-called Christian leaders who let them down.*

Most of those who will turn from their Christian walk were led astray by voices outside the local church, who predicted something that did not happen.

The apostles and prophets will now make their apologies, for the most part, and move on to the next prophetic event. The local pastors will be left to clean up, but the pastors' job just got harder. They must now try to convince their sheep that God's Word is still true. The local fellowship of believers is where they need to be attached and where God wants to bring a revival to their church and community.

I am a pastor, which is one of the reasons why this bothers me. For years, I have observed the behavior of the sheep. I have seen them pulled away from the local church by the glitter and glam of feel-good Christianity, scams, pyramid schemes, high-powered prophetic voices, and slandering words of malcontents. With every move detaching them from the local church, values are gradually watered down until a generation arises that knows nothing about God's ways.

All this points to a real crisis in the Body, particularly in our charismatic, prophetic movement. And it is not just a matter of the failed Trump prophecies. It is a matter of major necessary reform. What, exactly, should prophetic ministry look like in a New Testament setting? What's the difference between the gift of prophecy and a five-fold prophet? Should there even be a "prophetic movement" in the Church (as opposed to prophetic ministries serving side by side with teaching ministries and pastoral ministries)? What about accountability for false words? And how should prophetic words be filtered to the Body at large?

These are large and complex questions, questions that cannot be answered in isolation from one another. That means that only a mature, solidly charismatic, Word-based, Spirit-embracing, five-fold leader who is well connected with other respected leaders could write a book that would provide solid answers to these questions. That's why I'm thrilled that my friend and colleague, Dr. Joseph Mattera, has taken the time to write this urgently important book. Honestly, I could think of no one better to do it.

But Dr. Mattera is not here to tear down and destroy. If he does tear down, it is only to build something better, something more biblical, more God-glorifying, more edifying. If he exposes the false, it is only to exalt the true. He is no hyper-critic, presenting himself as the only one with right doctrine and practice, now set out on his latest heresy hunting mission. Instead, as an apostolic leader with a shepherd's heart, he is jealous for the health of the flock and eager to see Jesus exalted in the Church and in the world.

Proverbs states, "Open rebuke is better than love carefully concealed. Faithful are the wounds of a friend, but the kisses of an enemy are deceitful."[2] If the words of this book wound you, then embrace the pain and take the prescribed medicine. You will come out healthier than ever before. And if the words of this book give you fresh hope and faith, then ride that fresh wave of holy confidence. The Spirit is still speaking today!

The bad news is that spiritual malpractice is widespread in the charismatic Church today. The good news is that God is cleaning house. May all of us, then, get low in His sight. He resists the proud but gives grace to the humble. I, for one, need all the grace I can get.

Dr. Michael L. Brown
Host of the *Line of Fire* radio broadcast and author of *Playing with Holy Fire: A Wake-up Call to the Pentecostal-Charismatic Church*

---

2   Prov. 27:5-6

INTRODUCTION

My Christian walk started off with many prophetic signs and wonders that taught me the reality of the God who loves me, knows all about me, and determines my steps.[3] Even before I converted to Christianity, God answered my prayers of seeking in an extraordinary way to convince me of His reality.

Prior to my conversion, I always prayed and believed in God. However, like Cornelius of old, I was near the kingdom of God, but not in it.[4] In my teenage years, I was on my way to making it big in music as a guitar prodigy. However, God allowed me to go through a period of emptiness inside in which I found no satisfaction in anything I was doing, including my music. This resulted in a search for meaning and purpose.

My mother gave her life to Jesus when I was sixteen. Since her conversion, I attended a large charismatic church in the Bay Ridge area of Brooklyn with her on and off (more off than on!). After attending sporadically for three years, I wanted to know once and for all if what they preached was true. In November 1977, I asked my mother if there was a way I could live with "born again" Christians for a week. I wanted to determine whether or not they were just as sincere outside the church as they were in the church services.

She told me about a Full Gospel Businessmen's convention coming up in Washington, D.C. She told me I could spend a week with her and my uncle going to services. "There's a good chance you'll also meet some young people you can connect with," she said. I asked her how much it would cost.

"It's eighty dollars per person," she told me. I told her I did not have the money at that point. She told me she would pay for me, but I refused.

---

3   Prov. 3:5-8
4   Acts 10

"If God is real," I said, "then He would provide the money for me." That night, I prayed something like this, "God, if this 'born-again stuff' is real, please provide me with the eighty dollars to go to this retreat."

The convention was slated to start at the beginning of January. The convention got closer and closer, and I still had no money to attend. In those days, I was in three bands. One band was recording original music to present to record companies. Another was my college jazz band, and another was a wedding band I merely played to make money. Although our musicians in the wedding band were outstanding, the lead singer was awful and we always failed our auditions. Hence, at that point, I was broke!

With the convention looming, I received a phone call a few days after Christmas that our band received a gig on New Year's Eve because another band cancelled and the pay was—you guessed it—eighty dollars per person!

Consequently, I went to the convention and kept trying to connect with young people, praying to God to show me if Christianity was real. I loved the services, but I wondered about the sincerity of the Christians who looked so happy praising God in the meetings. After a few days, I got discouraged by something and I told my mother that I was going to take the train back home to New York. I got my luggage, went down to the lobby, sat down on a chair, and prayed, *God, if being "born again" is real and You want me to stay here, please send someone to me now to tell me about the way of salvation.*

I waited for 20 minutes, got upset, and said to myself, "This born-again stuff is not real." I picked up my luggage and walked out the hotel lobby doors, but something inside me told me, "Go back to where you were sitting." I turned around. Before I could sit down, a young man about my age named Michael Pierre came to me and asked me, "Are you saved?"

"I don't know," I answered him.

"If you don't know, then you are not saved," he said to me. Then he said, "Come with me, I am taking you out for dinner."

"Who sent you?" I asked.

"God sent me to show you the way of salvation." During dinner, Michael asked me if I believed Jesus died and rose for me. I replied yes. He then led me in the sinner's prayer, and I received Christ on January 10th, 1978. The next day I purchased my first Bible and began devouring it. I fully surrendered to the Lordship of Christ during a Sunday evening service the evening of the Superbowl, and the rest is history!

During the convention, Michael and his friends tried many times to get me "baptized in the Spirit" with the evidence of speaking in tongues, but I was not able to get past my intellect and human reasoning. However, at some point around August 1978, my mentor, Anthony, took me aside and explained in simple terms how to receive this "baptism of the Spirit." He laid hands upon me and the power of God came down. It felt as though a blanket of spiritual power had descended all over me, resulting in an inner sense of overwhelming joy which was released more and more as I spoke in an unknown language. I spoke in tongues in ecstasy throughout the night! However, before I left, he warned me, "This week, you will receive the greatest temptation you ever got thus far in your Christian walk." Confused, I asked him why he said that. He showed me the narrative of when Jesus was tempted in the wilderness by the devil after He was baptized in the Spirit (See Matthew 4).

The next night, after band practice, I got home at about ten p.m. and could not wait to study my Bible. Suddenly, I received a phone call from Marty, a fellow professional guitar player, who offered me a gig that would pay me $500 per week and take me all over the world. I asked if I could give him an answer the next day and hung up the phone, very confused and conflicted. I had practiced over six hours every day to establish myself as a world-class studio guitarist, and now the opportunity to make a real living playing music was in front of me.

Since the bulk of my time was spent studying the Bible and reading theological books, my prayer life was underdeveloped. Up until that point, I did not know how to hear the voice of God in my spirit. In desperation, I tried calling my mentor to get his advice, but his phone was constantly busy. I frantically prayed for God to tell me what to do, but there was silence. At eleven p.m., I calmed myself down and told myself that God wants me to walk in peace. As I picked up my Bible, I prayed one more time, "Lord, please show me if this offer is temptation from the devil." As soon as I prayed those words, the pages of the Bible opened up to Matthew 4 where the passage had the words "tempter" and "devil" highlighted in yellow.[5] I realized the devil was offering me the kingdoms of this world if I would only deny Christ.[6]

---

5   Matt. 4:3, 5
6   Matt. 4:8-10

Thankfully, once I knew it was temptation from the evil one, I was settled in my heart not to take the gig. The next morning, I called Marty and told him I was not interested. He was shocked and asked me if I had a better gig.

"Yes, I found a better gig," I said. Not long after that I quit all my bands, put down the guitar, and spent all my discretionary time reading the Bible and learning how to pray. Years later, when giving this testimony, I found out that members of that band eventually played with a world-famous songwriter. At least one of my old acquaintances continued for decades to be a part of his musical group, touring the world and making many hit records. I have no regrets and am thankful I made the correct decision by God's grace.

Fast forward a few years. While I was in Bible school, my future wife Joyce believed God spoke to her to go to the Moscow Olympics to evangelize in various Soviet communities. But at that point, she had no money to make the trip. However, that wasn't the only challenge she faced. The Communist government was not open to receiving missionaries. Under the tutelage of YWAM, she was encouraged to go with only one other person since it was too dangerous for teams.

In one of the prayer meetings Joyce attended, somebody prophesied over her that she would go to the Olympics with her husband. She wasn't dating anyone at the time, so she was a little incredulous at first. Being a firm believer that she needed to hear from God on her own and not be led by words of others, she went home and laid this word before the Lord, seeking Him for His will and guidance. In her prayer and devotional time, God confirmed that this was not the word of man, but indeed was from Him, and that she should continue her planning and not worry about the things He would bring to pass in His timing.

It was now the fall of 1979. Joyce still had no money, and was still not dating anyone, let alone marrying the man who would embark on this dangerous mission trip with her. In the meantime, she kept faithfully preparing for the trip and studying the Russian language. All her friends in her home group were concerned for her. They believed she was deceived and encouraged her to go for pastoral counseling because they thought she would have a nervous breakdown when the things God showed her did not come to pass!

Now, I had already become casual friends with Joyce, since we were in the same home Bible study group after I got saved. During the summer of 1979, I returned from a short-term mission trip to Turkey and knew nothing about what was going on. I went into the prayer meeting and felt a leading of the

Lord to lay hands upon Joyce. "God is going to fulfill His word that He spoke to you. Do not be discouraged or quit what you are believing for," I told her. After that, I became her only friend and confidant because I was not poisoned by her home group's gossip and skepticism.

As we spent more time together, I fell in love with her, and Anthony convinced me to propose to her. Thus, in January 1980, I asked her to marry me. She did not say yes or no right away, but we both agreed to fast and pray for three days alone and to come back and relate what we believe God said to us.

During those three days, I sought the Lord's guidance and pored over the Scriptures, trying to hear what He had to say. He directed me to Malachi 2:15, which says that God made them one so they can have godly offspring. As a fairly new believer who primarily read the New Testament, I had no idea that passage was in the Bible! To me, it seemed like a sign I was on the right path, but I would only know for sure when I talked to Joyce again.

At the end of our appointed time, we came back, and I asked Joyce if God spoke to her. She said yes. When we compared notes, we were blown away that God spoke to both of us the same way. He had given her the same passage, which bore witness to us that we should indeed get married.

We got engaged after only a few months of dating and got married on May 17th, 1980. We took all the money we received for our wedding and booked a six-week trip to Moscow, Leningrad, and Kiev that started right after the Moscow Olympics, since President Carter forbade Americans from participating in or going to the games. God moved powerfully in that trip with signs and wonders, resulting in the gospel going forth to hundreds of university students.

While in Kiev, we got caught leading people to Christ by spies of the KGB, so they started following us every time we left our hotel rooms. The maid outside our room would call down to the agents waiting for us outside the hotel entrance and they would follow us everywhere. We didn't want to get any Soviet citizens in trouble, and being followed hindered our ability to preach the gospel.

We got frustrated after a few days of this, and I told Joyce we wouldn't leave our hotel room until God spoke to us. After several hours of prayer and receiving no answer from God, I got impatient. "Let's leave the room now to go preach and see what happens," I said to Joyce.

As we were in the elevator, the Lord gave me an impression to go back to the room and continue praying. The time was not right. We went back and kept seeking the Lord. After about twenty minutes, I felt the Lord say, "Now is the time. Leave immediately!" So we left. The maid called down to the KGB agents, alerting them that we were on our way. As soon as the elevator opened, a huge truck pulled up with a large pile of luggage, temporarily blocking us from the view of the KGB officers outside the hotel. We hopped on a passing bus and immediately went to various places, preaching the gospel from under the noses of the KGB.

At the end of the day, we went to a popular public square where many English-speaking students hung out. The KGB knew we frequently went there to engage people with the gospel. After we garnered a crowd and began preaching, the KGB saw the crowd, approached us, looked right at us, and kept on walking in their search for us. Evidently, God blinded their eyes from recognizing us so we could continue to preach the gospel!

Fast forward to January 2017, I was with my son, Jason, his wife, Kendra, and some friends at a huge formal banquet. Jason and Kendra were struggling to conceive at the time, praying that God would give them children. During this event we met a well-known prophetic leader who said that he had a special faith to pray for barren women to have children. So I brought my son and daughter-in-law to meet him. We stood in a circle and prayed. The man suddenly laid his hands on them and prophesied, "This time next year, you will have twins." Well, just as he had prophesied, they had a beautiful set of twins! Asher and Ava were born in December 2017, and another set of twins named Olivia and Hunter came in July 2020.

My Christian journey started with God supernaturally confirming the gospel to me with His providence, and His specific ways of guiding me have continued to impact my life, the life of my family, and our local church. As a person thoroughly entrenched in both the evangelical and charismatic tradition, I hold to a high view of Scripture and attempt to build churches and movements with a balanced biblical perspective. Hence, the concern that comes forth saliently in this work is often an appeal for the prophetic and charismatic church to be biblically informed in both their orthodoxy and orthopraxy. I have given my life to the Lord Jesus Christ, who said that He is the one who builds His church.[7] As a co-laborer with Him, my work is focused on restoring the church to the way of Christ and His apostles.

---

7   Matt. 16:16-19

PART I

DEFINING THE FUNCTION
OF A NEW TESTAMENT PROPHET

CHAPTER 1

THE FUNCTION OF A PROPHET IN CONTEMPORARY TIMES

There has been much written about the function of the prophet in the past three decades. In this chapter, I will be writing regarding my own experience in understanding what the Bible says about the prophetic ministry, and I will attempt to connect this to today's world.

First of all, by the word "prophet," I am not referring to a person who exercises the gift of prophecy as taught in 1 Corinthians 14:2-4 (consisting of general exhortations, comfort and rebuke, which everyone in the church is encouraged to do; read 1 Corinthians 14:39). I am also not referring to a person preaching a sermon to a congregation. I am speaking about a person who, through much prayer, travail, and meditation in the Scriptures, hears and communicates what the Spirit is saying, to the church and (at rare times) the nation.

We have examples of a prophet standing in the council or court of the living God to hear His word in Isaiah 6:1-9; Ezekiel 1-3,10; and Jeremiah 15:19. Extraordinary New Testament examples of this can be found with the Apostle Paul in 2 Corinthians 12:1-12 and the Apostle John in Revelation 1:9-20 and 4:1-2. While very few people in church history have ever had similar existential encounters with the Lord and His heavenly hosts, those assigned to a prophetic ministry should at least have a robust prayer/worship life and be immersed in the Scriptures. Jeremiah 23:16-22 shows that the main distinction between false and true prophets is that false prophets speak without being in the council of the Lord and, hence, utter words without ever being sent by God.

I have found that, through my communion with the Holy Spirit, I can enter into a sort of mental and spiritual portal where I feel like I am actually living in the biblical narrative of the passage upon which I'm meditating. This meditation and communion is a crucial aspect of the prophetic. I believe that the prophetic gift is organically cultivated when a person regularly seeks the Lord and immerses themselves in the Word.

David Chilton says the following about prophets in his book, *The Days of Vengeance:*

> *The prophets not only observed the deliberations of the heavenly Council (cf. 1 Kings 22:19-22); they actually participated in them. Indeed, the Lord did nothing without consulting His prophets (Amos 3:7). This is why the characteristic activity of the Biblical prophet is intercession and mediation (cf. Gen. 18:16-33; 20:7, the first occurrence of the word prophet in Scripture). As members of the Council the prophets have freedom of speech with God, and are able to argue with Him, often persuading Him to change His mind (cf. Ex. 32:7-14; Amos 7:1-6). They are His friends, and so He speaks openly with them (Gen. 18:17; Ex. 33:11; 2 Chron. 20:7; Isa. 41:8; John 15:15). As images of fully redeemed Man, the prophets shared in God's glory, exercising dominion over the nations (cf. Jer. 1:10; 28:8), having been transfigured ethically (cf. Isa. 6:5-8) and physically (cf. Ex. 34:29). They thus resembled the angels of heaven, and so it is not surprising that the term angel (Heb. mal'ak, Greek angelos) is used to describe the Biblical prophet (cf. 2 Chron. 36:15-16; Hag. 1:13; Mai. 3:1; Matt. 11:10; 24:31; Luke 7:24; 9:52).*[8]

Prophets spend a lot of time cultivating an intimate relationship with the Lord so they can easily determine what God is saying to them and to their nation. Their relationship with the Lord allows them to discern what voices are not of God, separating the truth from the lies.

So how do those operating in the prophetic function in today's world? Prophets operate in today's world in ten main ways. First of all, prophets are

---

8   David Chilton, *The Days of Vengeance*, Dominion Press, 2006, p. 82.

people who regularly engage in deep intercession and travail for the purposes of God to be fulfilled on the earth. Whenever a person is in true Spirit-led travail of soul, they are literally participating with the council of God—pleading with God to have His way on the earth. A person who has no such deep experience with God will probably only be able to move in the simple gift of prophecy and not function in the office of prophet for the church.[9]

Secondly, true prophets take what they hear from God in the "Most Holy Place" and pray or pronounce the will of God by faith, so that His will is done, and His Kingdom comes on earth as it is in heaven.[10] Hence, what they speak in prayer is a divinely inspired order from God, which is then transmitted from the throne room to the angelic beings (both good and bad) who serve as the spiritual archetypes that influence the earth realm.[11]

Third, prophets can also be preachers who don't only come with prepared sermons based on human wisdom of words, but they may speak a specific word to the church and/or people that they heard from God's throne. This kind of preaching transforms individuals and congregations because the force and authority of the Holy Spirit is behind it and is manifest as a rhema word.[12] (Rhema is when God makes the spoken or written word real in the heart of the recipient.)

Fourth, prophets have a deep thirst to be in the presence of God and meditate on the word of God so they can actually engage God in the Scriptures while God burns His searing hot truth and light into their being. This in turn enables the prophet to understand how to apply the word of God to the people or situation he or she confronts, counsels or speaks into.

Fifth, prophets understand the times in which they live.[13] Through both natural knowledge (from reading newspapers, books, and interaction with high-level societal leaders) and spiritual knowledge (when in prayer or fellowship with God), they are able to take the natural knowledge they have assimilated and present it with clarity, divine accuracy and power. Thus, prophets not only read the Bible but also keep up with current events so they can apply the word to contemporary situations.

9   1 Cor. 14:2-4
10   Heb. 10:19; Luke 11:2
11   Matt. 18:18-19; Eph. 3:10
12   Heb. 4:11-13
13   1 Chron. 12:32

Sixth, prophets always have a window open to God in their souls, resulting in their consistent moving in words of knowledge, words of wisdom, discerning of spirits and prophecy, even when they are not engaged or totally focused on an act of prayer or in a church service or setting. Thus, they are always in fellowship with the person and presence of God and often hear what He is saying at a moment's notice, even in the midst of their mundane, daily activities.

An examination in the gospels shows that Jesus regularly moved in words of knowledge as part of His evangelistic and prophetic ministry, confirming His word to those He was speaking to.[14] I have often operated with this gift. Many times, the person I am speaking to doesn't know it because my words come in the context of a regular conversation, yet with significant results. I remember one time, when Joyce and I were driving back to the airport after a vacation, she noticed a store she wanted to shop in. While my wife was shopping, I started receiving prophetic words for the young lady who was trying to sell something to my wife. I started talking with her about her life in that city, and I began to share with her things I felt for her.

The next thing you know, this young woman was hugging me and crying about her life. I gave her my card and told her that if she ever wanted to get out of the city and come to New York, we would find her a place and help her. A few months later, she took me up on the offer and we got her settled with another couple. Soon after, she found out she was pregnant. If she was not with us and going to our church, she would have aborted the baby. Eventually, a young couple in our church who could not conceive adopted her baby, who is now a brilliant, handsome, talented young man living for the Lord. This young lady eventually enlisted in the military. Because she spoke several languages, she ended up working closely with the special forces.

For another example, one time while I was driving my car, I received an impression in my spirit that a person serving in a local high-level community board position was supposed to run for political office. I made an appointment to meet with her and told her what I felt and she broke down crying, telling me she had been wondering if she should do this. Consequently, she ran for office and won. We became close friends and she is one of the leading elected officials in our community and city.

---

14   Mark 2:8-10; 3:17; John 4

Seventh, prophets do not necessarily have to be pastors or preachers, but they can be marketplace leaders who function with a high degree of intimacy with God. They then use the word God gives them in profound ways to engage culture and affect change in the lives of those they are working with. For example, read Daniel 2, 4, and 5 and the account of Joseph in Genesis 40-41. These are two men who functioned in a secular assignment but utilized their prophetic callings to transform nations and empires. For a contemporary example, I have a prophetic friend, Hubie Synn, who is not a pastor but makes a living as an accountant. One day, while he was at an airport, he felt an impression to give a prophetic word to a Jewish man regarding a book he was writing. That person turned out to be world-famous author Jonathan Cahn, who was praying about the book at the moment my friend gave him that word. That book, *The Harbinger,* became a national best seller.

Eighth, prophets walk in the royal favor of God. Somehow, they are usually at the right place at the right time. God is always providentially opening up doors for them or guiding them, even when they are not aware of it! We see this in Philip's chance encounter with the Ethiopian eunuch on the way to Gaza.[15]

Ninth, prophets have the spiritual insight to interpret the redemptive reasons for the suffering, pain, and seasons of life that people experience. They give profound words of advice that can transform a life, answer a prayer, bring clarity to an enigma, or help a person discover their purpose, just with a short conversation, prayer, or prophetic word. Whole books of the Bible like Isaiah, Jeremiah, and Amos illustrate the power of prophets who can interpret the times and the seasons for their people and their nation.

Tenth, in the Old Testament, prophets were called to represent God to a people or nation and bring a covenant lawsuit to them.[16] The word "witness" was originally a legal term regarding a person that was an aide to a person bringing a lawsuit. Thus, prophets who stood in the heavenly council as witnesses of the Lord not only heard God's will regarding a people or nation, but could actually be part of the process that brings judgment to that person or people group.

In the church today, anointed intersession can be a way of participating with God's heavenly council by prophetically praying and or speaking out the will and intention of God.

---

15   Acts 8:26-40
16   Mic. 3:8

Biblical examples of this participating with God in the execution of His judgment on the earth include Elijah declaring to King Ahab that Israel would have a drought until his word released rain; Peter pronouncing judgment upon Ananias and Sapphira for lying; Paul blinding Elymas the sorcerer for obstructing the gospel; and John bearing witness to the words of Christ that resulted in bringing judgment on false Israel and the pagan systems of the world that Israel aligned itself with.[17] Most importantly, prophets have learned that those who are friends with politicians and wealthy people are a dime a dozen, but those who are intimate with God are very few on the earth. The most important function for a true prophet is to be a friend of God who knows Yahweh and speaks to Him "face-to-face" as a man speaks to his friend.[18]

Due to the fact that apostles and prophets are usually listed together as co-laborers in the New Testament, there is a need to compare these two ministry functions for the sake of clarity.[19] But what is the difference between the two?

---

17   1 Kings 17:1; Acts 5, 13; Rev. 1:3

18   Deut. 34:10; John 15:15

19   1 Cor. 12:28; Eph. 2:20, 4:11

CHAPTER 2

THE DIFFERENCE BETWEEN APOSTOLIC AND PROPHETIC FUNCTIONS

Although the Body of Christ has been growing more in relation to understanding the missional role of APEST, there is still a lack of clarity regarding the difference between apostolic and prophetic function.[20] APEST is an acronym for the functions of Apostle, Prophet, Pastor, Teacher and Evangelist, as listed in Ephesians 4:11. (For more on the APEST gifts, see chapters 15 and 16.) When we examine the Scriptures regarding the apostolic and prophetic functions, we find only a slight difference regarding ability in executive leadership roles; the main difference is the actual ministerial expression of leadership ability.

Many view prophetic ministers as folks who merely float from one place to the next as itinerant ministers who give "words of the Lord" to individuals and organizations, but have little or no ability to lead large, effective organizations. This definition is not sufficient in light of biblical teaching and models. Ministers who function like this may very well be "exhorters" who have a prophetic edge rather than functioning as a New Testament type of prophet. To explore why this distinction exists, we first need to look at the Old Testament.

Apostolic Archetypes in the Old Testament

The main difference between the ministry of Prophet in the Old Testament and New Testament is the fact that Old Testament prophets received

---

20   Eph. 4:11

direct visions and dreams from God.[21] Thus, there was no room for error. However, in the New Testament, "we [only] know in part and prophesy in part," which is why all prophecies should be judged by mature leaders.[22]

Even in the contemporary church, God still uses apostles to be the foundation of His church as those whom He calls to plant churches and lead movements of churches.[23] Jesus started and established His church—also called a nation—with twelve men He called apostles.[24] When using the Old Testament as our guide, we find that many of the men called "prophets" were serving in roles that most today would consider "apostolic." Men like Abraham, Moses, and Samuel who were called prophets in the Old Testament would certainly be called apostolic leaders if they were functioning in the same capacity today. For example, Abraham was a patriarchal leader who was the progenitor of a whole nation and the recipient of a covenant with God. Samuel was not only a prophet, but a judge and civic ruler of Israel.[25] Moses, also called a prophet in Deuteronomy 18:15, would certainly be considered an apostle today. He was the main person God used to establish the nation of Israel, including their ceremonial and moral laws and a system of government to rule several million people.[26]

Furthermore, one could argue that Old Testament prophets were the equivalent of New Testament apostles with no real difference in function or calling. Ephesians 2:20 tells us the church has been "built upon the foundation of the apostles and prophets." We could say the word "prophets" in this passage is not referring to New Testament apostle/prophet teams but only to Old Testament prophets, since the New Covenant was based upon the prophetic writings handed down from the patriarchs. (This is a position I generally agree with, although 1 Cor. 12:28 seems to put these two ministerial functions as a foundation for local churches.)

Acts 13:1-2 teaches that the great first-century church in Antioch was led by prophets and teachers, with no mention of apostles in that church. This shatters the false assumption that present-day prophetic leaders are merely

21 Num. 12:1-8; Ezek. 13:1-7
22 1 Thess. 13:9; 1 Thess. 5:19-21; 1 Cor. 14:29
23 1 Cor. 12:28
24 1 Pet. 2:8-9
25 Gen. 12:1-3; 15:8-17; 17:4-8
26 Ex. 18:17-27; Ex. 20-25

trans-local exhorters that cannot lead huge organizations or networks. If we find no real separation between the governmental nature and abilities of apostles and prophets, then why separate apostolic and prophetic ministerial functions, as we see in 1 Corinthians 12:28 and Ephesians 4:11? As we examine the Scriptures, perhaps the real reason for this New Testament separation lies in the fact that, in the Old Testament, prophets were mainly called to minister in a single geographic location, as God was building a theocratic-model nation in Israel. So, even though prophets were sent, they were mainly stationary regarding their national focus.[27]

Apostles, on the other hand, were deployed as God's missional leaders to be His witnesses throughout the world.[28] This view goes along with the nature of the title "apostle," which literally means "a sent one." This term was taken from the Roman army, which called generals sent to set up beachheads in enemy territory "apostles." Since the resurrection of Christ, we now have powerful leaders with anointings to go where Christ has not been named or where there is no real kingdom witness to set up beachhead *ekklesias* (that is, congregations called out by God) as salt and light to establish God's kingdom in every nation and sphere of life.

If this is true, then many people we today call "apostolic" are really New Testament prophetic leaders, and many of those we call "prophets" are merely exhorters who have a mature gift of prophecy as described in 1 Corinthians 14:3. There are also far fewer apostolic leaders among the ranks of self-proclaimed "apostles." I remember when I stepped into apostolic function for the first time. This episode began a significant shift in my life from prophetic to apostolic ministry. I was about thirty-three years old. I had been scheduled to teach a group of pastors in the Dominican Republic around the spring of 1992. The seminar in Santo Domingo was based on a "school of the prophets" I had been doing in New York City and beyond. I had traveled as a prophetic minister, participated in prophetic presbytery (when several prophetic leaders take turns prophesying over individuals chosen by their pastor in a local church), and launched a prophetic team as part of an apostolic network. However, as I was preparing the day before the seminar, I had a strong sense in my spirit that I was supposed to teach on "apostolic

---

27   Is. 6:6-9

28   Acts 1:8-9

networks" instead. Thus, I wrote out my notes and discarded my plans to teach on the prophetic.

The next day, I saw God move more powerfully than ever before. I introduced the apostolic to about fifty pastors. After a few hours of teaching, I knew I would be wasting my time if we did not immediately put into practice the concepts I was sharing. During the lunch break, I spoke to three of the key leaders I sensed were present and told them that I felt like we were supposed to launch an "apostolic network" for their city. I proposed who I felt the leader should be, as well as his surrounding apostolic team. These leaders bore witness to it, and at some point in the seminar I shared the prophetic word I had, proposing the launch of a new apostolic network. Everybody affirmed this, and the Dominican Republic's first apostolic network. This network of pastors and leaders eventually became the largest in that nation. Last I checked, it was still going strong twenty-five years later!

I mentored the main apostolic leader and spoke into that nation for several years, walking alongside Jim Jorgenson, a prophetic elder whose family we sent to live there for five years. He continued to build relationships and advance the kingdom mightily in that nation. The main difference between apostolic and prophetic leaders is minute, having to do with style and mode of operation. When apostolic leaders engage in problem-solving, teaching, or strategizing, they tend to speak more out of principle—out of the accumulation of their vast storehouse of wisdom and experience. In contrast, prophetic leaders engaging in the same kind of problem-solving have a different mode of delivery, based more on receiving a spontaneous "word of the Lord" or prophetic utterance.

However, these different modes of ministry are necessary and vital to the Church. Both work in tandem to establish a kingdom witness on the earth. Both can be involved in laying the foundation of a local church and in building a network of churches and establishing organizations. While prophets may tend to speak into an already-established entity, apostles tend to be the initial leaders in establishing said entities. Both are necessary; the apostle for pioneering new territory and order in unreached areas, and prophets for bringing fire, passion, and a continual sense of urgency into the faith communities of those entities established by apostles.

In saying this, it would be a huge mistake to imply that apostolic leaders are not prophetic. On the contrary, apostolic leaders must be extremely prophetic because, when being sent to lay a foundation and establish a beachhead for God in new territory, they must receive a word from God in regard to the timing, the geographic location, and the strategic spiritual warfare needed to be successful in their missions. Those functioning apostolically must always have an acute sense of the Lord's leading. Hence, apostolic leaders must have profound prophetic ability. Their primary focus of their ministries is simply on the management, development, and administration of leadership and the establishment of church government, whereas prophetic leaders have as their primary focus the renewal and continued movement towards hitting the mark in regard to corporate purpose and power.

Based on the realities presented above, perhaps there are more apostolic and prophetic leaders working together than we think. Moreover, maybe it is not just those we deem apostles, but also true prophetic leaders who tend to shy away from some of the more extravagant, showy, shallow itinerant prophetic ministers out there today. True New Testament prophets are so principle-centered they cannot relate to trans-local ministers who merely exhort, make prophetic proclamations, and then leave with little to no accountability or oversight. True New Testament prophetic leaders are builders, not just blessers, and as such, there may not be such a great present-day divide between apostolic and prophetic leaders. After all, many apostolic leaders are married to prophetic spouses!

As we come to the next chapter, we'll expand the definition of the prophetic function to include the marketplace. In the New Testament, there was no artificial bifurcation between the church and the workplace, since local churches met in people's homes or apartments. The faith was integrated in such a way that, as we read the book of Acts, most of the activities of the Spirit took place outside the four walls of a building. We will also explore the difference between what I call "Kingdom prophets" and "church prophets." Both are absolutely necessary for Kingdom expansion.

CHAPTER 3

THE DIFFERENCE BETWEEN KINGDOM AND CHURCH PROPHETS

We in the Charismatic expression of the Body of Christ have had much teaching on prophetic ministry since the 1980's, including some good teaching that brought clarity and balance, but also some other teachings reaching toward the extreme. All in all, when examining Scripture, I find one area lacking in regard to prophetic emphasis, and that is the narrow focus of prophetic ministry to only those in the Church. There has been some powerful prophetic ministry via preaching, exhortation, and sharing what people have heard from God's heart, either for individuals or for the nation. But most of it has only been heard by other church people, and it rarely—if ever—goes outside the four walls of a church building.

This was not how the prophets of the Old Testament or the New Testament functioned. If the Old Testament is to serve as our primary model for how the original prophets influenced culture, then it is clear from a cursory examination of Scripture that prophets didn't just prophesy in the temple or a synagogue. The prophets of Israel were called to speak the word of the Lord to cultural elites who were positioned to guide the nation. Daniel served as a top political advisor to the King Nebuchadnezzar of Babylon and as a prime minister in Persia, which positioned him to speak truth to power and transform the Babylonian and Persian nations.[29] Nehemiah was the cup bearer of the King of Persia, which gave him the favor necessary to rebuild the walls of

---

29   Dan. 1-6

Jerusalem.[30] Samuel, first in the line of great Jewish prophets, also served as the political judge of the nation.[31] His protégé David may have been a great prophet and psalmist, but he also became Israel's greatest king.[32] The prophet Elisha ministered even to the Gentiles in Syria.[33] These prophets had political and cultural access to the most powerful people in the world. Thus, their prophecies had immediate impact. The prophetic words of Old Testament prophets had the potential to reach the primary decision makers of nations, unlike the prophecies given today, which are only voiced on Christian media outlets or in church services.

For example, Elijah not only prophesied to a poor widow but also to King Ahab.[34] He also anointed a person to serve as king in a foreign nation.[35] Elisha, the spiritual son of Elijah, ministered not only to the kings of Israel and Judah, but also to the Gentile nation of Syria, Israel's enemy.[36] Political kings even referred to Elisha as "father" and to themselves as his "sons".[37]

Even in the New Testament, prophets were called to influence the world around them. When we examine it, we see how the apostle Paul reached some of the elite citizens of strategic cities.[38] For example, he ministered to a top political official named Sergius Paulus in Paphos, Cyprus.[39] In Philippi, he preached to Lydia, a rich merchant, and he reached many of the leading women of Thessalonica.[40] He built relationships with Priscilla and Aquilla, who had their own tent-making business in Corinth and Erastus the treasurer of Rome.[41] We also see him testifying to governors Felix and Festus, King Agrippa, and the leading men in Malta in accordance with his original com-

---

30   Neh. 1-2
31   1 Sam. 3:10
32   1 Sam. 16-2 Samuel 3
33   2 Kings 5:1-14; 8:7-10
34   1 Kings 17:10-16; chaps. 18-19
35   1 Kings 19:15
36   2 Kings 3:6-27; 6:8-23; 5:1-14; 8:7-10
37   2 Kings 6:21; 8:9
38   Acts 10-11
39   Acts 13
40   Acts 16; 17:4
41   Acts 18; Rom. 16:23

mission.[42] Church history also tells us that Paul eventually appeared before Caesar Nero and preached the gospel at least once or twice before he was executed.[43]

I see the prophetic going outside the four walls of the church next, just as it was with the biblical prophets. We have made a slight improvement in this area with a greater understanding of "prophetic evangelism," in which we go up to strangers and share with them things from the heart of God that only He knows about them, drawing many people to Christ. There have also been some instances when prophetic leaders have ministered to high-level political leaders, but regarding expectations of prophetic leaders in the church, this has been the exception, not the rule.

I have personally stepped into this realm with high-level political leaders as a bishop in New York City, which enabled me to pray with and share the gospel with many elected officials. This has included giving the word of the Lord to a community leader (that I barely knew) that they were supposed to run for a particular powerful office. They cried and said they were just thinking about whether they should do it. They didn't mention it to anyone else. This person ran and won the election! But this hasn't always led to victory on the politician's part. On several occasions, I felt the Lord told me to warn top political leaders and predicted their demotion for deviating away from biblical ethics in their policies. Several of those leaders lost their positions and were even arrested!

While leading a multi-ethnic socio-political coalition, there were also times where we frequented the state capitol, continually meeting and reasoning with senators, assemblymen, and elected officials related to our objectives. One time, when these leaders met in the Senate chamber for an all-day debate, the Lord gave me so much favor that I was able to walk in and out of the chamber, giving senators the word of the Lord in conversation. Some of the coalition leaders were shocked at the amazing access I had, but that came from years of befriending the senators and working closely with them for the good of the city.

We are now coming to a place where the Church's understanding of being the salt and light of the world will impact all our planning for ministry

---

42   Acts 23-28; Acts 9:15

43   2 Tim. 4:16-17

and vocation, in which all of society will be our parish. Not including the public realms of society in the prophetic and missional focus of the Church will perpetuate a dualism in which the Church builds mega-subcultures that neither embrace surrounding communities nor engage secular society. This results in Christians prophesying and having conversations with themselves.

I am not saying we don't need church prophets or that church prophets are bad. Prophets were essential and arguably the primary people God used to transform culture, and I believe it is still the model God wants to use to influence nations. We just need to expand our thinking enough on prophets' incredible calling to include an important aspect of the prophetic call to culture.

The ultimate aim of prophecy—whether to kings or to Christians—is to lift up the Lordship of Christ overall and to advance the gospel. When ministering to presidents and kings, generally prophetic words should point to the Lordship of Christ. Like Paul's model, it should involve preaching the gospel under the inspiration of the Spirit.[44] It should not always involve giving advice regarding partisan politics. As we saw in the 2020 election, it has catastrophic results and brings dishonor to the prophetic movement, especially when it came to a preponderance of prophetic voices predicting Donald Trump would win a second term in office. Not only did these prophecies *not* come to pass on election day, but several of these prophets insisted the Lord told them that Donald Trump would be installed on Inauguration Day. When that did not come to pass, some said the military would install Mr. Trump in early March, which still has yet to happen. We are still waiting for many of these prophetic leaders to apologize for this mistake that misled untold thousands of social media followers. Not only that, these prophetic mistakes were done with an arrogant spirit, equating their words with the mouth of God Himself. When time elapsed and proved their words were not spoken by the Lord, it was a public embarrassment, causing confusion within the Church and mockery outside the Church.

Furthermore, this excessive focus on election fraud disputes distracted Christians from putting their time and money toward the spread of the Gospel. One leader told me that one marketplace leader told him that a million dollars went towards the legal battle for Trump to remain in office

---

44   1 Cor. 12:3; Acts 24:25; Acts 26:4-30

after he lost on Election Day. Consequently, much money that was promised towards Gospel initiatives was diverted elsewhere. I believe many people gave partially because they believed the prophetic words that Trump was supposed to remain in office, which was dependent upon proof of voter fraud in a court of law.

In spite of all these challenges, it should not discourage the church from using the gift of prophecy outside the church building. Let's examine the prophetic calling in the context of one's community and vocational assignment.

Contrasts Between the New Emerging Kingdom Prophets and Church Prophets

- Kingdom prophets speak the heart of God for all of life; church prophets speak regarding only church life.

While the most common expression of biblical prophecy and inspired preaching is done in the context of the local church, we see the prophets throughout the Scriptures speaking truth to power in the public square, not merely within the confines of the temple or church edifice.[45] Old Testament prophets and leaders such as Moses, Isaiah, Jeremiah, Amos, and Daniel spoke to the kings and rulers of their day. Paul the Apostle preached to Roman governors, as well as King Agrippa.[46]

- Kingdom prophets mentor kings and princes of the earth; church prophets mentor other church prophets, intercessors, and leaders.

I believe that the Old Testament was given to the church as an example of how we can function as Christ followers in the context of our new life in Christ. Thus, the Old Testament is also a guidepost when it comes to how God operates through His people in contemporary culture, serving as examples to us in the New Testament epoch.[47] We see Old Testament prophets, such as Elisha, advising and functioning as a spiritual father to kings.[48]

45 1 Cor. 14
46 Acts 24-26
47 1 Cor. 10:6
48 2 Kings 8:7-15

I have also functioned much in this capacity in my own community and city. For decades, I served as one of the primary religious leaders to many of the major elected officials, community board, and police. I had personal contact with them, gave them advice, and prayed with them. In our state, I have often gone to the capitol during crucial seasons related to family policy and held many press conferences on steps of City Hall. Consequently, I have found that it is crucial for spiritual leaders to be a voice into elected officials. Most of them desire this and wonder why representatives of His kingdom are often absent from the halls of power.

- Kingdom prophets influence those who can shift a global culture; church prophets influence those who can shift congregations and networks within a church's subculture.

On my website, my tagline is "Influencing leaders who influence culture." I have discovered that many significant leaders in the Church and in the workplace read my weekly articles and use them as a teaching and mentoring tool in their own context. I don't even know how many of these people even got on our newsletter list! However, when someone with vast influence in the culture has their thinking impacted by my writing, I know this is a kingdom function related to my prophetic calling.

- Kingdom prophets have a marketplace assignment to influence whole communities; church prophets prophesy to church movements and individuals.

From 1981 to 1995, my wife Joyce and I felt compelled to stay in our particular community as church planters. We spent many days in fasting, had powerful corporate prayer gatherings on a regular basis, and heard the word of the Lord related to what He was calling us to do next in our region. Joyce launched a large non-profit charity related to education, family life, and beyond to aid thousands of children. Many of these children have also heard the gospel when attending church services. Our team also worked hard to present the gospel through puppet shows, skits, and movies to our neighbors in street meetings. After over a decade doing this, we eventually noticed a total shift in the atmosphere and quality of life for the 160 thousand residents of Sunset Park community—all without gentrification. Consequently, we have discovered that the gospel is able to not only lift individuals but whole communities.

- Kingdom prophets have learned to speak the language of secular culture; church prophets speak the language of religion.

I teach those I mentor in our church and family to "think biblically and to speak secularly," as Alan Platt says.[49] If we are going to have influence in the public arena, we cannot merely quote Bible verses to elected officials and community leaders. Many of those in our church have gone on to have vast influence, like my son Jason, who uses the biblical worldview as his foundation for hundreds of public debates on television and radio. This would not have happened had he not learned to speak the language of culture.

Of course, most pastors and church leaders are primarily assigned to their particular congregation, which is fine. Since the Church is the "pillar and ground of the truth," it is the most important institution in the world to influence culture.[50] If the church is "out of whack," then there is no hope for their surrounding culture or nation.

- Kingdom prophets often have access to governmental buildings; church prophets have favor in pastors' personal offices.

Many of my colleagues and friends have had enormous access to both Democratic and Republican presidents. A close pastor friend of mine with a solid biblical worldview is constantly on the phone with the past two mayors of New York City as an advisor of current affairs. Evangelist Billy Graham was a personal friend of several U.S. presidents and spoke into nearly every president from Eisenhower's presidency in the 1950's up until Graham's death a few years ago.

---

49   Alan Platt. "Prepare Kids to for Leading, Not Just Following," AlanPlatt.org (blog), August 19, 2014, https://www.alanplatt.org/article/identity-in-christ/prepare-kids-for-leading-not-just-following.

50   1 Tim. 3:15

- Kingdom prophets speak regarding the Lordship of Christ over societal currents and trends; church prophets prophesy about church-related issues and events.

At times, Kingdom prophets may have a strong personal relationship with the Lord. For instance, Dr. Martin Luther King, Jr. functioned as a Kingdom prophet as he utilized Christ's non-violent methods to advance civil rights in America. However, God does not confine His work to those who know Him, but He may use people outside the Church to bring about His will. Because of God's common grace (not to be confused with saving grace), which He gives to both the Christian and non-Christian to keep the world functional, He uses certain people for His glory for His own purposes to be fulfilled in the world.[51]

For instance, God raised up Persian King Cyrus as His anointed vessel to accomplish His work, even though Cyrus did not know the Lord.[52] In the twentieth century, we saw a great secular prophet with the rise of Winston Churchill, who warned the world for many years about Adolf Hitler and the rise of Nazi Fascism. God used both men to alter human history for their generation!

- Kingdom prophets influence the climate of a community or city; church prophets influence the atmosphere of a church service and congregation.

I have witnessed great prophetic leaders minister the word of the Lord and shift the atmosphere in a church service. In the same way, Kingdom prophets can influence important public policy decisions for a community, city, or nation through their relationships with elected officials and community leaders.

For a personal example, I remember working for a few years with a prominent assemblyman in my community related to limiting the porn industry and other quality of life issues. He would run legislation by me, conduct press conferences with me, and participate in my marches and rallies. Every

---

51   Matt. 5:45; Eph. 2:8-10
52   Is. 45-46

community needs spiritual leaders and Kingdom prophets to represent His Kingdom if we are going to express God's wisdom practically for the world.

- Kingdom prophets feel comfortable befriending marketplace leaders; church prophets focus on befriending committed church attendees.

God graces Kingdom prophets in high levels of the marketplace. Friends of mine who function as Kingdom prophets seamlessly move in these spaces. In non-profits I have connected with, we have worked with Hollywood celebrities, professional athletes, and other major marketplace leaders through our common goal of serving communities. I feel as comfortable in these spaces as I do in ministering and interacting in church spheres.

I also worked for a few years with a senator to connect a hundred pastors and non-profit leaders with state officials in "My Community and Us," an initiative that connected faith-based leaders with state officials to partner in serving their city.

As we examine both testaments of Scripture, we should view all this as normative Kingdom work. Nehemiah worked with King Artaxerxes of Persia to get a government grant to rebuild the wall of Jerusalem.[53]

- Kingdom prophets father political and economic kings; church prophets father leaders in church life.

My greatest joy in life is to serve as a father. In addition to having five biological children, my wife and I have numerous spiritual children in our church and beyond. I have also served as a mentor and spiritual father to numerous marketplace leaders with huge influence in their communities. I have found that once marketplace leaders have the correct spiritual alignment, their workplace influence and resources can explode!

- Kingdom prophets train cultural leaders; church prophets train church leaders.

---

53 Neh. 1-2

As part of our call to influence culture, in the late 1990s I started the "Ekklesia Leadership Institute". Once a month, I took the young people with the most potential aside and poured into them in three-hour sessions. The results were amazing! One of my spiritual daughters, in response to her desire to influence culture, became a lawyer and married a person who became the legislative director for the RNC. Jason, one of my biological sons, turned his liberal college upside down, became the public relations spokesperson of Young America's Foundation, had his own national radio show, appeared regularly on various television shows, and wrote two *New York Times* bestselling books—all by age 27!

In the early 2000s, I spent three years training young leaders and pastors from about sixty churches in the Empire State Building location of a local Christian college. This greatly impacted hundreds of people, giving them a biblical worldview and inspiring pastors and churches to engage their communities with love and wisdom for the glory of God.

- Kingdom prophets can serve as elders in a city; church prophets can serve as elders in a local congregation.

As a voice for the Kingdom, I knew I was called to be a shepherd to my community, not just our congregation. For many years I served as one of the primary spiritual leaders of my community. Whenever the police had an issue, I would mediate between them and our local elected officials in my office. I would open up in prayer at our annual festivals. I was asked to be part of the regional crisis management team with the NYPD after the tragedy of September 11th and served on the community board for three years.

As the lead pastor of Resurrection Church, I also served as the lead elder for our oversight team. I saw no bifurcation, compromise, or conflict in these dual roles, since the earth is the Lord's and the fullness thereof![54]

- Kingdom prophets are gifted with all the learning and knowledge of contemporary culture; church prophets are gifted with all the learning of church dogma and doctrine.

---

54   Ps. 24:1a, KJV.

Kingdom prophets spend a lot of time reading newspapers and analyzing current trends and thoughts as futurists who are called to understand the times in which they live, just like the sons of Issachar.[55] This is the only way they can have the heart and mind of God for their generation. Combining this knowledge with a robust prayer and devotional life, they can interpret the times and the seasons and tell God's people how they ought to respond as the "salt" and "light of the world."[56]

- Kingdom prophets are respected and are visible in mainstream media outlets; church prophets are famous only in Christian media outlets.

God has many believers in every space of society. God's Kingdom is represented in people who have a large platform, whether they are film producers and distributors in Hollywood, sports analysts, political commentators, or professional athletes. I have even heard of influential Bible studies causing Gospel permeation among Big Tech industry staff.

God has His celebrities, professionals, and people inside the halls of power that He grants a platform for His purposes. In the book of Esther, we can also see a great example of this. A young lady, Esther, won a national beauty contest and became the Queen of Persia. This ascension to the throne allowed her to step in and save the Jews from a genocidal plot.

All of Scripture, including the Old Testament, is given to us as a model on how we ought to live out our faith.[57] I believe we will see the fullness of this cultural prophetic call in the next few decades as the church continues to grapple with and grow in cultural engagement. I also see an incredible move of God as more and more prophetic and apostolic leaders speak the word of the Lord over leaders of developing countries in Africa, Latin America, and even Asia. Let's believe God for the Church to nurture leaders who will not only be respected and quoted in Christian magazines, but also publish editorials in the *New York Times, The Washington Post,* and other major global news outlets.

When the church attempts to go outside the realm of the local church to prophesy, there will be some significant learning curves, as well as huge

---

55   1 Chron. 12:32
56   Matt. 5:13-14
57   1 Cor. 10:11; Rom. 15:4

mistakes in the process. This isn't the time to quit, but to continue to study the Scriptures, get advice from mature seasoned leaders, and continue to use the prophetic to influence every arena of life for the glory of God.

PART II

THE PERVERSION OF THE CONTEMPORARY PROPHETIC MOVEMENT

CHAPTER 4

THE DAY OF RECKONING HAS COME

I adhere to the continualist movement of believers who belong to the Pentecostal, Charismatic, and Third Wave tradition. As a continualist, I function in the gifts of the Spirit, including the gift of personal prophecy.[58] I have been burdened about the state of the prophetic for several years. However, I have become increasingly alarmed due to the prophecies and practices of those associated with the prophetic movement. Furthermore, since the beginning of 2020, many public national prophecies have not come to pass, which has added to my growing concern.

Deuteronomy 18:22 tells us, "[W]hen a prophet speaks in the name of the Lord, if the thing does not happen or come to pass, that is the thing which the Lord has not spoken; the prophet has spoken it erroneously…" The prediction that COVID-19 would quickly dissipate right after the Passover and the re-election of Donald Trump are two such erroneous prophecies. But even so, these errors have significant results. I was part of a prophetic panel in early April 2020 in which approximately eighty percent of the prophetic voices predicted COVID-19 would lift quickly and that Trump would be re-elected. (I was not part of that eighty percent.) What has made it worse is that even after President Trump's controversial loss on election day, several high-level prophetic voices have continued to contend that he will remain in office. While prophetic voices such as Shawn Bolz, Jeremiah Johnson, and Kris Vallotton have already made public apologies

---

58   1 Cor. 12:5-8

for missing it, others, such as Kat Kerr, Johnny Enlow,[59] Hank and Brenda Kunneman, Kenneth Copeland[60], and many others were still contending throughout January 2021 that Trump would remain president through divine intervention.

Consequently, Joe Biden has since been inaugurated as America's new President. The day of reckoning has come for many in the prophetic movement. Judgment begins first in the house of God.[61] While many conservative Christians focused only on Donald Trump's re-election, God uncovered the sick, shallow underbelly of the contemporary prophetic movement. What good is the re-election of a conservative president if a large portion of the conservative Evangelical church is biblically illiterate and lacks spiritual discernment? They are easily sucked into conspiracy theories and shallow, politically driven prophetic words that are not grounded in the fundamental principles of Scripture. This has publicly humiliated the prophetic. It's as bad as the numerous warnings wrongly predicting the looming bodily return of Jesus within a generation of Israel's birth as a nation in 1948.[62]

Truly, as of January 21, 2021, there is a crisis in the charismatic world. What is needed in the charismatic/prophetic church is introspection and repentance. We need to repent for:

Prophesying out of a subconscious mind instead of through the sovereign spirit of God.

These prophets obviously cannot discern the difference between their human soul/spirit and the Spirit of God.[63]

Prophesying out of their political bias and the lens of so-called "Christian nationalism."

---

59   Right Wing Watch *(@RightWingWatch)*. *"Right Wing Watch Twitter Post." Twitter, January 15, 2021, https://twitter.com/RightWingWatch/status/1350119615934902277?s=20.*

60   Spocchia, Gino, "Kenneth Copeland Laughs Maniacally at Media for Calling US Election for Biden," *The Independent*, November 9, 2020, https://www.independent.co.uk/news/world/americas/us-election-2020/kenneth-copeland-biden-trump-election-b1719273.html.

61   1 Pet. 4:17

62   Hal Lindsey, *The Late Great Planet Earth*, (Grand Rapids: Zondervan Academic, 1970).

63   Jer. 23:16

The Bible teaches us that we know in part and prophesy in part.[64] Hence, we all prophesy out of the lens of our own experience, knowledge, and worldview. I believe that many of the pro-Trump prophetic voices were motivated by their impulse towards various forms of "Christian nationalism." By "Christian nationalism," I am referring to the belief that key settlers of the New World made a covenant with God to represent Him and bless the world, which some believe is similar to the covenant God made with Israel, although God initiated the covenant with Abram for the birth of Israel—not vice versa.[65] I have heard it said numerous times that America is the only nation that made a covenant with God during its founding besides Israel. Although I believe God had a particular plan to use America to spread the gospel and bless the world, it was never entirely a Christian nation. This is obvious from our blighted history, starting with legalized slavery.

Furthermore, God has a plan for Jesus to inherit all nations, not just the United States.[66] Only individuals can be a Christian; nations as a whole have no such ability.[67] However, as the salt of the earth, it is proper for all believers to influence a nation's laws so a Christian ethos can be reflected in its policies. This results in a country having a culture favorable to Christian values.

Going to God to get a word rather than prioritizing time with God to discern His ways.

One of my concerns is that too many contemporary prophetic voices seemed to be going to God merely to "release a word" to their online audience instead of plumbing the depths of God to know and communicate His ways. The Old Testament prophets and New Testament apostles focused on knowing God's ways. This is evident in Psalm 25:4, Jeremiah 9:23-24, Hosea 6:3, John 17:3, and Philippians 3:8-12. Knowing God's ways is much more important than merely going to God for a prophetic word. When we go to God for a word, we are merely using God to advance our self-interests. God desires that we seek Him for His sake because we delight in Him. This is the only way to mature as a Christ-follower.[68]

---

64 1 Cor. 13:9

65 Gen. 15; Heb. 6:13-20

66 Ps. 2:8-9

67 John 3:3-8

68 Ps. 37:4; Ps. 42; Ps. 63; Ps. 103:8

Equating their prophecies with the canon of Scripture.

Only the Scriptures are purely God-breathed.[69] Thus, no other words or experiences are equal to the surer word of prophecy, which is the compilation of sacred writings we now call the Bible.[70] Contrary to these teachings, many of these prophets demand people believe their word as if it was the word of God Himself. This is erroneously encouraged, even though we are clearly instructed in the New Testament to judge prophetic words and to test the spirits.[71] Even the greatest prophets merely prophesy in part and know in part.[72]

Over-reliance upon visions and dreams.

In the Old Testament, God primarily spoke to the prophets through visions and dreams.[73] However, in the New Testament, dreams were usually used for guidance before the Spirit was poured out upon the Church (i.e., God leading Joseph in dreams, as shown in Matthew 1-2). Peter quoted the prophet Joel on the Day of Pentecost and stated that, among other things, one sign of the New Covenant age was that "your old men would dream dreams."[74] We see only two significant instances related to guidance by a vision and or dream in the post-Ascension: when the Apostle Paul was led to Macedonia, and when the Spirit instructed the Apostle Peter through a vision not to call Gentiles unclean anymore, though it's unclear whether the latter was an open physical vision or spiritual vision.[75] I have also heard that prophetic leaders such as the deceased Bob Jones moved accurately in prophetic dreams, as well as some other credible contemporary prophetic leaders that people in the Charismatic church vouch for. That said, most of the time, the leading of the Lord took place by the Holy Spirit collectively speaking to the Church or through the individual's spirit.[76]

Equating themselves with the Old Testament prophets.

---

69   2 Tim. 3:16-17

70   2 Pet. 1:19-21

71   1 Cor. 14:29; 1 Thess. 5:19-21; 1 John 14:3

72   1 Cor. 13:9

73   Num. 12:1-8; Ezek. 1

74   Joel 2:28; Acts 2:14-21

75   Acts 10; 16:9

76   Acts 13:2; 15:28; 16:7-8; 1 Cor. 2:10-14; Rom. 8:14-16

Since God spoke verbatim through the Old Testament prophets, belief in prophetic words was equal to belief in God's word.[77] However, this is no longer the case in the New Testament.[78] It is a hermeneutical mistake to quote 2 Chronicles 20:20 for present-day prophecies. In the New Testament, we only prophesy in part and are required to test prophecies before we believe and act upon them.[79]

Using the gift of prophecy to influence the national election.

The primary use for prophecy is to glorify God by edifying the Church.[80] I have found that very few prophetic voices are consistently accurate when they go beyond personal prophecies and attempt to give prophecies for a nation. Of course, New Testament prophets and apostles *can* prophesy regarding the fate of kingdoms and nations, but only a select few are called to do this.[81] The ones outside these few are usually prophesying beyond their level of authority and faith.[82] Prophecies must also align with the Lordship of Christ, according to 1 Corinthians 12:3. The spirit of prophecy should always be the testimony of Jesus.[83]

Even in the Old Testament, prophecies of nations were spoken through the lens of their relation to the plan and purpose of Jesus Christ.[84] Since Jesus is inheriting all nations, I believe prophetic words from Him are still needed regarding their alignment with His Lordship.[85] However, these words should not be rife with mere political motivations.

Falling into mass prophetic delusion through group think.

Similar to instances when the majority of the Old Testament prophets prophesied what they believed was good for their nation instead of the true word of the Lord, some of today's prophets have fed off one another and fallen into a corporate spirit of deception. This is similar to the situation we see in 1

---

77   2 Chron. 20:20

78   Heb. 1:1-2

79   1 Cor. 13:9; 1 Thess. 5:19-21

80   1 Cor. 14:2-4

81   Acts 11:27-29; Rev. 10:11

82   Rom. 12:7

83   Rev. 19:10

84   1 Pet. 1:11

85   Ps. 110:1-2; Eph. 1:10

Kings 22, when Jehoshaphat and Ahab sought the Lord's guidance in going to war against Ramoth Gilead. Four hundred prophets prophesied that the Lord would bring about victory for the Israelite kings, but only Micaiah prophesied that the other prophets were told to lead Ahab to his death in battle.[86]

This is exactly what's going on today. It can happen again, but it doesn't have to. We must not be swayed by what everyone else thinks would be best for our country.

Engaging in QAnon predictions as a presupposition for prophetic words.

It is almost hard for me to believe, but I was informed by several mature prophetic leaders that many in their camp are influenced by QAnon posts. The Bible blames the human dilemma on sin, while QAnon blames all societal evil on a secret cabal of Democrats who are supposedly involved with human trafficking.[87] QAnon is a cryptic conspiracy theory that originated on the dark web. It is anonymous and often wrong; hence, it violates many of the basic principles of the word of God. Scripture admonishes us to "know those who labor among us," to have nothing to do with anything done in darkness, and to judge all words given.[88] How can we judge an anonymous source?

THE SIGNIFICANT CONSEQUENCES

Unfortunately, many of the erroneous prophetic words have influenced millions of naive, sincere Christians, who longed to see the candidate of their choice get elected so he could "save the republic." There most likely will be dire consequences for them unless they have strong pastoral guidance. (Woe to those who are not in a mature Gospel-centered church!)

Some possible consequences are:

Masses of rank-and-file naive Christians being disillusioned with the charismatic gifts.

It would not surprise me that one major backlash from these misleading prophecies is that tens of thousands of Christians will leave the Charismatic

---

86   1 Kings 22:1-40.

87   Rom. 3:23.

88   1 Thess. 5:12; Eph. 5:11; 1 Cor. 14:29.

movement (especially churches that strongly espoused the prophetic) and turn instead to cessationist Christian expressions of the Church. My concern here is that cessationist churches tend to limit the gifts of the Spirit in the lives of the congregation, thus hurting their ability to edify one another in the faith. Even worse, many may even become disillusioned with Christianity itself if their faith was intrinsically integrated with the prophetic. Hence, when these false prophetic words were deconstructed after January 20, there will be a popular concomitant deconstruction of these leaders' shallow grasp of the gospel.

Movements built upon the prophetic will be shaken to their core.

There are some Charismatic networks and movements that have totally bought into the prophetic excess mentioned in this article. Those networks will likely have seismic aftershocks that may even threaten their very existence in the future if they do not honestly repent and make immediate changes. Many pastors, leaders, and church members may disassociate with networks who don't strongly correct the latest examples of prophetic excess. When there is a substantial exodus, it significantly affects these networks' finances and forces them to re-focus and evaluate their methods and mission, leading to a massive overhaul.

Young prophetic leaders will separate from some of their older prophetic mentors/peers.

In my experience, younger evangelicals generally eschew extreme political connections to Christianity. That said, it is possible that many young leaders in the prophetic movement will distance themselves from both their movement and their mentors. They will not want to be connected to those who made false national prophecies and those who aligned themselves with conspiracy theorists and far-right activists.

The secular world will lump all Evangelicals and Charismatics together.

As is always the case, the world will also attempt to excoriate all Christians (especially white conservative evangelicals) because a minority of them publicly went along with conspiracy theories and prophetic-type activism. There have already been exposés by major secular newspapers like *The Washington Post, The New York Times,* and beyond.

The world will question the validity of all our historic beliefs.

The world will likely be inclined to question the validity of all the beliefs of those who confidently prophesied things that did not come to pass. Unfortunately, this includes the historic belief in the death, burial, and resurrection of Jesus Christ; He is our only hope and is Himself the gospel. This will make it even harder to witness to those who still need Him.

May mature apostolic/prophetic voices arise today! May they eschew unbiblical practices. May they guide the Charismatic Church into a glorious future that will see the advancement of His kingdom.

CHAPTER 5

WHY MANY PROPHETIC VOICES DID NOT HAVE 2020 VISION

The year 2020 was ushered in with a cornucopia of prophetic utterances. However, it quickly became evident that many of the more popular prophetic voices fell short in their prophetic declarations. For example, many prophets missed it when they prophesied COVID would suddenly dissipate right after Passover. Because of the magnitude of the challenges 2020 brought, their lack of accuracy was magnified for all to see.

Now, in light of the election debacle, the prophets who declared that President Trump was going to win a second term (some even added that he would win by a landslide) are being seen in a negative light. As a result, their followers have raised questions about the legitimacy of their prophetic leaders.

As a shepherd and a leader in the Body of Christ, my heart is not to condemn or criticize those who have missed it prophetically, but it is for the Church to be unified.[89] Given the prophetic mistakes that have occurred, I'm concerned about the potential division and confusion within the Body. Because of these inaccurate prophecies, some may give up on the gifts of the Spirit, leave charismatic churches, or worse yet, completely backslide.

In the New Testament, Paul admonishes believers to judge and test prophetic words. This implies that there is room for error and leniency.[90]

---

89   Jn. 17:20-33.
90   1 Thess. 5:19-21; 1 Cor. 14:29

Furthermore, Romans teaches that mature sons of God are led by the Spirit of God since the Holy Spirit is within each believer.[91] In contrast, the Old Testament prophets had no room for error. God gave them dreams or visions containing direct messages from Him.[92] In those days, they were the only ones who had direct communication with the Lord, so when the prophets delivered a message from the Lord, it was the same as if the Lord Himself were speaking to the people. One can read Hebrews 1:1-2 for the fundamental difference between Old Testament and New Testament prophets. God now speaks corporately to the church in His Son as opposed to limiting His oracles to the prophets in the Old Testament. Thus, when some of the contemporary prophets quote 2 Chronicles 20:20 to encourage people to believe their predictions, it is not exegetically applicable in the post-resurrection New Testament. Hence, the Church is presently not to be led only by prophets, but believers are to discern both individually and corporately what the Spirit is saying to the churches.[93]

WHY PROPHETIC VOICES SOMETIMES MAKE MISTAKES:

They prophesy out of their human spirit.

Jeremiah 23 is key to understanding the nature of true and false prophetic words. God did not say that all erroneous prophetic utterances are the result of a demonic spirit. Essentially, God said that many prophets speak out of their human spirit instead of God's heart and mind.[94] These prophets did not distinguish between their souls and their spirit. Instead, they spoke out of their own emotions or biases.

They listen to lying or seducing spirits.

The apostle John admonished the church to test the spirits since not all spirits proceed from God.[95] However, 1 Kings 22 shows us that God sometimes allows corporate lying spirits to speak through prophetic people. This is to test people to see whether they will take heed to mature prophetic

---

91   Rom. 8:9, 14
92   Num. 12:6
93   Rev. 2:11
94   Jer. 23:16
95   1 Jn. 1:1-4

voices who are grounded in the word of God or whether people will instead choose to listen to false prophets who merely prophesy to appease the masses. However, to be fair, in this passage, the lying spirits were likely put into the mouth of those who did not follow Yahweh.

They prophesy to their base.

1 Kings 22 also illustrates how prophetic voices can sometimes get caught up in crowd-pleasing and playing to their base. For example, traveling prophets can sometimes fall into the temptation of flattering the senior pastor with glowing prophetic words. For example, they may prophesy about revival coming to the church with the hope that they will be invited back to preach.

In the narrative of the book of Jeremiah, there was continual pressure upon Jeremiah to prophesy peace and prosperity. Instead, he predicted the looming captivity of Jerusalem. As a result, he was continually rejected and persecuted for his prophetic declarations. Since many prophetic voices had a huge following of Trump supporters, whether they realize it or not, they can be tempted to utter words conducive to what their base wants to hear.

They prophesy beyond their level of faith.

Romans 12:6 teaches us to prophesy according to the measure of our faith. Whenever we give a word that transcends our spiritual maturity and or faith level, we go from being inspired to being soulish. Some prophetic leaders are continually tempted to give huge elaborate words beyond their spiritual capacity because they seek to gain more followers and enlarge their platform.

They are not held accountable for their mistakes.

After the huge COVID debacle, I have not heard any prophetic leader admit they made a mistake, nor did I hear anyone else calling them out and holding them accountable for their mistake. I chose to keep my powder dry and did not specifically call people out concerning this, as I did not want to embarrass my brothers in the Lord. Any one of us can make a mistake once in a while. However, it's imperative for those who miss it prophetically to receive correction. If a person is not open to correction, then he can become a danger to the Body of Christ. That person should also be encouraged to refrain from releasing public prophetic words until he or she submits to recognized seasoned leaders in the Body of Christ.

The bottom line is, if the word fails to come to pass, it was not a genuine word from the Lord. Knowing that any of us can make a mistake, it may be prudent for us never to say, "Thus says the Lord" when we give a word. Instead, we can say something like, "I believe the Lord is saying…" so others may feel invited to test the word for themselves. When a person says, "God told me…" or "Thus says the Lord…" they become their own canon and make it harder for others to judge them, since it can sound like they are judging God Himself. A great lesson for the contemporary prophetic movement is found in Jeremiah 32:6-8. In this snapshot, the great biblical prophet Jeremiah tests his own prophecy before he declared it was from God.

They go beyond their lane of assignment.

Many prophetic voices are very accurate when giving personal prophetic words but are inconsistent when it comes to giving national words. Just because a person functions with an accurate "simple gift of prophecy" within the local church doesn't mean they are called to give national prophetic words.[96] When they go outside of their lane, they will often make mistakes and give false hope to their followers.

They continually feel the pressure to attract followers.

Unfortunately, there is a human tendency to feel pressure to continually perform up to a certain standard. Such performance often garners followers, which sometimes translates to bigger offerings, and a larger social media platform. In addition, this drive to perform expresses itself in giving spectacular words to compete with other prophetic voices.

They copy the words of other prophetic voices.[97]

In 1 Kings 22 and in the book of Jeremiah, we see that there is often a consensus of a particular company of prophets who echo the same general prophetic narrative: a national victory over their pagan adversaries. In light of this, there may be peer pressure for other prophets to conform to the most popular and influential voices among them. When this happens, group discernment collapses down to the initial prophetic voice who has the most influence.

96   1 Cor. 14:2-4
97   Jer. 23:30

However, even if there is consensus among the prophetic voices, one should dig further and investigate if the prophetic voices declared something independently of one another and if they did so without knowledge of previous prophetic words. Otherwise, they can all be guilty of practicing groupthink and falling into a herd mentality which dissipates the genuine, pure word of the Lord.

Their paradigm and theological bent influence their prophetic words.

1 Corinthians 13:9 says, "…we know in part and we prophesy in part." By implication, this suggests that all prophetic words are filtered through the lens of the prophetic person's knowledge and assumptions. Our prophetic words are shaped by our worldview, eschatology, and human experience, as well as our political bent. Therefore, we need other members of the Body of Christ with a different perspective to judge our words. For example, those with a conservative political lens may have a proclivity to prophesy victory for conservative candidates. Those who prefer big government intervention may slant their prophetic words towards candidates and policies with a socialist perspective.

Nobody is exempt from personal biases. No one is entirely pure when giving prophetic utterances. Only the Holy Spirit speaks with complete accuracy one hundred percent of the time. Cultural nuances and current events do not move the Holy Spirit.

My prayer is that this will be a time when God uses this crisis to mature His Church. In addition, may the Holy Spirit increase our biblical discernment and capacity to move in spiritual gifts so that His Kingdom advances.

One of the biggest hindrances to prophetic advancement and maturity is the rise of social media prophets. This is because unproven, unknown people can garner a huge audience merely by dropping prophetic words that appeal to undiscerning masses of people. We will unpack this in the following chapter.

CHAPTER 6

THE RISE OF SOCIAL MEDIA PROPHETS

Since the mid-twentieth century, we have seen the medium of communication go from a dependency upon the printed book to broadcasting via radio and TV to the present digital age. The results have been nothing short of a seismic shift related to the amount of access the average person has to unlimited voices and information. This has served to be both a blessing and a curse.

It is a blessing because more pertinent information related to every subject is now available to the masses. As recently as two decades ago, the Evangelical church was influenced by only a small collective of prominent voices such as James Dobson, Pat Robertson, Tony Evans, Billy Graham, and more, who could sway the Evangelical church politically and doctrinally with their teachings on radio and TV. But now there are multitudes of Christian influencers who have garnered a huge following because of media-savvy content. It no longer takes a budget of millions of dollars to attract a wide audience, which means anyone can share whatever message they want to.

Out of this "flat earth" Christian milieu, there are now numerous self-proclaimed prophets proclaiming what they say is "the word of the Lord" to both the Body of Christ and to the nations. While many of these prophetic people may be sincere Christ followers (some are also charlatans doing it for filthy lucre), the biblical way to disseminate personal prophetic words is in the context of the local church gathering, especially so mature prophetic leaders can judge said word. This method of vetting words is vital for the health and safety of the church and ensures proper pastoral application of the word to the recipient.

Related to this vetting principle, the apostle Paul said the following, "Let two or three prophets speak, and let the others judge".[98] Furthermore, Paul taught all the manifestations of the Spirit, including prophecy, in the context of the local church gathering—which included the observance of the Lord's supper.[99] Hence, the healthy and biblical practice of the gift of prophecy should have a corporate dynamic.

Unfortunately, in spite of these clear instructions in the New Testament, I have heard of numerous people in the Body of Christ following so-called Internet prophets that now find themselves with the ability to reach a huge audience—without paying the price of being vetted as a mature leader in a local congregation.[100] Although we don't know their life, their track record, personal ethics, the state of their marriage and family, and their accountability structure, they can deliver a purported prophecy that excites and inspires multitudes. Furthermore, many of these same people are promoting "prophetic events" via social media by offering "a word of the Lord" to all who attend, while at the same time bypassing the local church and the spiritual leaders God has assigned to shepherd the naive believer enticed to these events because they are constantly on Facebook, Instagram, and other mediums of media.

Not that long ago, a certain prophetic voice started using their social media platform to hold meetings in a hotel in New York City. Prophetic words were given to people from other churches, including our church, without their pastor-elders or mature leaders being present to judge said words. I spoke to one of the leaders facilitating these events and, thankfully, they apologized and stopped these meetings. They were just ignorant of the proper biblical procedures related to conducting prophetic ministry. I wish all the prophetic leaders were as open and accountable as this person was!

The writer of Hebrews said, "Obey those who rule over you, and be submissive, for they watch out for your souls, as those who must give account. Let them do this with joy and not with grief, for that would be unprofitable for you."[101] With all the strange teachings, questionable doctrines, and

---

98   1 Cor. 14:29
99   1 Cor. 11:17-14:40
100 1 Tim. 3:1-12
101 Heb. 13:17

unaccountable prophetic voices prevalent today, it is increasingly difficult for contemporary shepherds of local churches to faithfully feed the flock because of the plethora of cacophonous voices in and to the church today.

The only recourse for shepherds of churches is to continue to be faithful by consistently teaching the Word, making disciples, and preaching the whole counsel of God both in public gatherings and in-house meetings. This is the only way the sheep can have more discernment and flee from unaccountable prophetic leaders and strange doctrines that incite questions rather than godly edification.[102]

May all nine manifestations of the Spirit flourish for the edification of the Body of Christ, so Jesus will be glorified in His Church, amen. (Read about how the nine manifestations of the Holy Spirit were taught in the context of the local church in 1 Corinthians 12:4-27.)

Finally, since there are now so many unvetted platforms for prophetic voices, it behooves the church to be able to discern the difference between "rogue" and "real" prophets.

---

102   Acts 20:25-32; 1 Tim. 1:3-7; Heb. 13:9

CHAPTER 7

DISCERNING BETWEEN ROGUE AND REAL PROPHETIC MINISTRIES

As stated in the previous chapter, there has been a huge rise in the past several years of prophetic ministries and leaders appealing to masses of believers via social media, instead of through local churches, by promising them personal "prophetic ministry." This troubles me on several levels, since many of the people attending these conferences are not seasoned leaders of churches, but are people lacking biblical depth and discernment.

In my nearly forty years of pastoring, I have learned that if you want to fill up a room, you promote an event by giving the impression that everyone has a chance to receive personal prophetic words. (Or give away free pizza!) This is a far cry from the late 1940s, when the prophetic movement had a resurgence. In those days, a prophetic presbytery made up of three to five seasoned leaders would offer ministry, judging each other's words as a team of elders prayed over the people looking for a word from the Lord. The recipients of said ministry were expected to fast and pray for several days before they received it. Now, many attend conferences without their pastor and or church elder and receive "personal words" from trans-local ministers without the authority or the pastoral oversight these people need to walk out these words practically. This is different, of course, from pastors and seasoned leaders gathering for mutual edification, instruction, and prophetic ministry. Of course, there is still the need to judge the prophetic words they give to one another as elders. However, even in this case, prophetic words should be recorded as well as judged by competent leaders to protect both the prophet and the recipient and ensure the meaning of the prophecy comes through clearly.

When we examine prophetic ministry in the New Testament, the best guide is from Paul's first epistle to the Corinthians. Most prophecies are merely an expression of the simple gift of prophecy as described in 1 Corinthians 14:3, which says, "…one who prophesies speaks to men for edification, exhortation and consolation."[103] In this context, Paul says that all believers should "desire spiritual gifts," especially that they prophesy, since prophecy "edifies the church."[104] Since this is a gift all should crave (even as Moses also alluded to in Numbers 11:29), this is different from those whose primary ascension gift ministry is that of the prophet as described in Ephesians 4:11-16.

That is to say, since many people can operate freely with the simple gift of prophecy, like many in these rogue movements, many unfortunately eventually confer upon themselves the so-called "office of prophet" even though they lack the experience, leadership, anointing, and calling of the Ephesians 4:11 ascension gift of Prophet. The office or ministry function of prophet is not to be claimed by all who have the simple gift of prophecy as found in 1 Corinthians 14:3, since all Christians are encouraged to operate in this gift, while the Ephesians 4:11 gift of the prophet is only for some based on their specific assignment in the church place and workplace according to the context of these two passages.

Those who function in the ministry gift of the prophet should serve in a foundational ministry that includes oversight and governance, according to various Scripture references.[105] However, some of these prophetic conferences gathering crowds to receive "words" have folks unattached, unaccountable, and disconnected from a local church. The average immature believer is mesmerized by the prophetic due to their lack of maturity in the word and Spirit necessary to discern the voice of the Lord for themselves. Therefore, before a person goes to a so-called "prophetic conference," they should first find out what group these "prophetic people" belong to, what church they attend, what leadership role they have in a local church, who they are accountable

---

103   1 Cor. 14:3, NASB
104   1 Cor. 14:1, 4, NASB
105   1 Cor. 12:28; Eph. 2:20; Eph. 4:11-12; Acts 13:1-2

to, and who their oversight is. Without understanding these foundational questions, it is foolish and even dangerous to sit under these ministries. It is also unwise to receive prophetic ministry without your local church elder, mentor, or pastor present to judge and help apply and interpret said word.

In the context of Paul's instructions in 1 Corinthians 14, prophecy should be given to edify the church—not to disconnect people from their church, and not apart from their local church. The simple gift of prophecy works best in a house meeting, a small group environment, or during a local church assembly, if it is to function according to the biblical pattern. The local church is usually a safer environment than rogue conferences (or parking lots) because prophetic words can be judged by other leaders and trusted prophetic people.[106]

Of course, this is vastly different from prophetic evangelism, which was the primary methodology Jesus employed when He ministered the Good News to others. He usually walked in the spiritual gifts of the word of knowledge and wisdom when speaking to others, which helped authenticate His ministry in the minds of those who met Him.[107] Thus, when ministering to strangers we meet in an airport, on the street, or working out in the gym, there is nothing wrong with moving in the prophetic gifts outside of a church service like Jesus did to demonstrate to people the reality of the God who sees, knows, and loves them.

In light of this, we have to learn to differentiate between prophetic evangelism for salvation or edification to strangers we may never see again and the use of prophecy as a vehicle to edify and equip individuals in the context of the Church, and we must learn the proper biblical protocols for each.

Last but not least, Paul's guidelines related to the use of spiritual gifts all focus on the corporate function of believers as Christ's body, which illustrates the fact that all spiritual gifts are given to edify the church.[108] They are never given as mere individual words to satisfy a person's craving for individual destiny and fulfillment. Thus, this individualistic expression of the prophetic doesn't align with Scripture, but is instead a construct of rugged American individualistic Christianity that trumps individual desire above the wellbeing of the Body of Christ.

---

106   1 Cor. 14:29
107   1 Cor. 12:4-8; John 1:46-49; John 4:16-19
108   1 Cor. 12-14; Eph. 4:11-16

Furthermore, there is really no such thing as "personal prophecy," since all prophecy to individuals found in both the Old and New Testament had ramifications related to their assignment. They call to either the nation of Israel, in the case of the Old Testament, or for the furtherance of the Gospel through the local church.

I pray that these simple instructions will convict those utilizing their simple gift of prophecy to gather crowds, influence, and, in some cases, for mere monetary gain. I also pray this serves as a useful guideline pastors can use to equip and mature Christ followers under their care, so the sheep are not misled, scattered, and unattached from His Body which is His church.

As we move into the next chapter, we delve into the dark underside of the prophetic. Some use their prophetic gifts to manipulate others. Thus, it is important for the church to understand the difference between manipulation and edification in the prophetic.

CHAPTER 8

DISCERNING BETWEEN PROPHETIC EDIFICATION AND MANIPULATION

The Bible teaches us that true prophecy edifies the church and also exalts the Lord Jesus Christ.[109] However, where there are true prophetic gifts, there are also counterfeits and the wrong use of God-given gifts. For example, in the Scriptures, we see that the prophet Balaam tried to use his gift for financial gain.[110] Even though his motives weren't godly, Balaam still had a bona fide prophetic gift.

I have personally witnessed prophetic ministry used to manipulate others into making business decisions, coaxing a congregation to raise money to purchase a building, and winning over wealthy people for filthy lucre. One so-called prophet even sells his words for a price as high as five thousand dollars. However, one of the most common examples of manipulation I have witnessed is when a person gets "a word" that someone they are attracted to is supposed to marry them. The bottom line is all prophetic gifts have to be framed by the intent, motives, and ultimate purpose of the written Word. People can use their prophetic gifts either for edification or manipulation.

Contrasts Between Prophetic Edification and Manipulation

Prophetic edification benefits the church, building her up in the faith. Manipulation benefits only the prophet by calling attention to himself. At

---

109   1 Cor. 12:3-7; 14:3-4
110   Num. 22:21-39

worst, a manipulative prophet can coerce the person receiving the word in doing or believing something that does not come from the heart of God.[111]

Prophetic edification exalts the Lord Jesus. Manipulation exalts the one giving the prophetic word.[112] All true prophecy should exalt the Lord Jesus because the ministry function of the Holy Spirit is to point to Jesus and glorify Him.[113] When a person giving a prophecy exalts or points back to themselves, it is a sign they are not expressing the mind and heart of God.

Prophetic edification advances God's Kingdom.[114] Manipulation advances the ministry of the prophet. True prophecy should ultimately motivate the recipient of the word to serve the Lord for the glory of His kingdom and purpose. If a prophecy points back to serving the prophet, then a red flag should immediately go up.

Prophetic edification advances the vision of the church. Manipulation advances the financial gain of the prophet.[115] I have seen traveling prophets come into a church and flatter people with grandiose words, like calling them an "apostle," or telling them that they will be sent out as a "prophet to the nations." Thus, these kind of prophets have no vision for the house of God and rarely ever prophesy a word that will solidify their commitment to their local church. Sometimes they will even flatter the lead pastor with a great prophecy of revival coming through their congregation with a hope they will get a larger offering and be invited back to speak. They may even give a flattering word to those they deem to have the most money in the hope that they will stay in touch with the person, eventually leading to regular financial support.

Prophetic edification points people to the vision of the church. Manipulation draws people away from the church towards the prophet (Acts 20:30).

Prophetic edification builds the spirit. Manipulation entices the unredeemed ambitions and unresolved issues in the emotions of the hearer (Ephesians 5:18-19). Even false prophets can intuit insecurity, selfish ambition, and a critical spirit in people sitting in church. They can easily take advantage of these broken places in people and prophesy things that play right into

---

111   1 Cor. 14:4
112   1 Cor. 12:3
113   John 15:26
114   Matt. 6:33
115   Num. 22; Rev. 2:14

their unredeemed ambition and emotions to get them excited and willing to support and follow the prophet who "understands" them!

Prophetic edification builds discernment. Manipulation takes advantage of naivety in the believer (Proverbs 1:2-4; Romans 16:18). True prophetic ministry will enable the recipient of the word to understand clearer the mind and will of God for their life.

Prophetic edification is motivated by God's agenda. Manipulation is motivated by the prophet's agenda (1 Kings 22; Jeremiah 23).

Prophetic edification is accountable to spiritual authority. Manipulation is accountable to no one (1 Corinthians 14:29). Every person who gives a prophetic word should be willing for other mature prophetic people and leaders to judge the word. Prophets who carry a spirit of manipulation submit in their heart to no one but themselves.

Prophetic edification is built upon a correct handling of the Scriptures. Manipulation is built upon a distortion of the Scriptures (2 Timothy 3:16-17, 4:3; 2 Peter 2:1). All true prophecies should be aligned with the words of the Bible. Anything that distorts the truth of the Word is not a genuine word of the Lord.

Prophetic edification gives us great faith in God. Manipulation gives us great faith in the prophet (John 7:18). Whenever I have been in the presence of true prophetic ministry, the whole atmosphere is charged with faith. When there is a spirit of hype, emotion, and manipulation, it only points to the prophet and doesn't build up the people of God.

Prophetic edification emanates from the Counsel of the Lord. Manipulation comes from the imagination of the prophet (Jeremiah 23). True prophetic ministry represents the will and reign of God emanating from His throne, where He deliberates decisions with His heavenly council. Manipulative prophecy originates not with the mind of the Lord, but from the subconscious and desire of the prophet.

Prophetic edification expresses the heart and mind of God. Manipulation expresses the desires of the prophet (Jeremiah 7:24).

Prophetic edification speaks the truth in love. Manipulation flatters for personal gain (2 Peter 2:18).

Prophetic edification helps to mature people in the church. Manipulation eventually drives people out of the church (Colossians 1:28-29; Acts 15:32). Manipulative prophecy can eventually drive people out of the Church because the recipients of the word often blame the Church if fleshly prophetic words don't come to pass. They may also leave because these false prophecies discourage them, leading to disillusionment in their faith.

Prophetic edification motivates people to seek the Lord. Manipulation motivates people to seek the prophet (Isaiah 55:6-7). True prophetic ministry should give us a hunger to seek God even more. Prophecy is the testimony of Jesus, not of the prophet (Revelation 19:10).

Prophetic edification implores people to confirm the prophetic word. Manipulation scares people into being led by their word (2 Corinthians 13:1). Manipulative prophecy often puts fear in the hearts of the hearers, which can cause them to act presumptuously to fulfill said word in the strength of their own flesh.

Prophetic edification encourages humility. Manipulation encourages selfish ambition (Isaiah 57:15; Philippians 2:1-12).

Prophetic edification seeks the honor of God alone. Manipulation seeks glory from men (John 7:18).

Prophetic edification has an eternal effect. Manipulation has a temporary effect (1 Peter 1:25).

Prophetic edification builds up the hearer. Manipulation takes advantage of the hearer (Ephesians 4:29).

My desire is that pastors and leaders can use these simple propositional statements to develop discernment in the Church, increasing accuracy and influence and the conformity of prophetic people to the will of God.

As we move on to the next chapter, we will do a deeper dive into the unhealthy, questionable prophetic practices currently tolerated in the charismatic church.

CHAPTER 9
THIRTEEN QUESTIONABLE PROPHETIC PRACTICES

Though my experience has been overwhelmingly positive, in nearly forty years of prophetic ministry I have witnessed the good, the bad, and the ugly! As I was musing over prophetic ministry for this section, I thought a lot about practices that are either harmful or manipulative. This list is to encourage best practices for the edification of the local church and beyond.

Questionable Prophetic Practices:

1. Unaccountable prophets

I have learned never to invite a prophetic leader to minister if I do not know who they are aligned with. Before I send an invitation, I need to know: Who do they have to mediate if a sin or moral violation is uncovered in their life? One of the most dangerous weapons in the hand of our enemy is an anointed leader who is not accountable to anybody else.

2. Individualistic prophetic words

Most prophecies, both in the Old and New Testaments, were usually given in the context of the assembly of the Lord. There was no such thing as "individual destiny," "individual vision," or personal prophecies, or words isolated from the context of either Israel or the Church. Even words given to individuals in the Old Testament were either directly or indirectly related to the recipient's assignment for the nation of Israel.

In the New Testament, Paul the apostle enumerates in detail the gifts of the Spirit—including prophecy—in the context of Holy Communion, discerning the church, and with the understanding of the corporate Body of Christ. Paul explains the manifestations of the Spirit in 1 Corinthians 12:4-8. The surrounding context of this passage demands that the gifts are used to edify the Church. Chapter 11 lays out housekeeping rules for Communion, a corporate practice, and the gifts listed in 12:4-8 are then explicated corporately in 1 Corinthians 12:12-30, and applied and judged by other prophetic people in the assembly, as seen in 1 Corinthians 14:29. We cannot separate the operation of the gifts in 1 Corinthians 12 from the description of Communion, or the teaching on love in chapter 13. The gifts are intentionally sandwiched between these chapters that focus on Christian unity so that nobody thinks they can go off and utilize the gifts and power of God for their own advantage and gain.

3. Flattering words

I have seen prophetic people come into churches and flatter the pastor and other key leaders in the church. Whether it was motivated intentionally or unconsciously, I don't know. I cannot tell you how many pastors I have met who claimed they received a prophetic word declaring them to be "an apostle" and or that their church will be "the congregation to usher revival into their region." These kinds of words excite the congregation and the pastor, but unfortunately, most of the time the only result is another invitation for that prophet to come back. And if said words do not come to pass, the prophet can always get off the hook by stating, "The prophetic words are always conditional upon the faith and obedience of the recipients."

A word of caution about this: we all need to be careful and wary of prophetic voices who put all the blame of unfulfilled words they give on a lack of faith in the recipients of the word. It only brings condemnation, guilt, and shame to sincere people who think they failed God because some awe-inspiring word spoken over their life did not come to pass. Of course, most prophecies are conditional based upon obedience to God, but at the same token we have to have discernment regarding the motive and method of people who are always in the habit of giving glorious prophecies to people that rarely come to pass.

4. Soulish words

I have seen some people in my own local church prophesy out of their own soul based on internal issues they were grappling with that they attempted to put on the rest of the church. In addition, I have witnessed people prophesy to the church that which was personally troubling them and or convicting them and instead of recognizing that the word was solely for them, they spoke it out to the church. In essence, they denied the word was for them and tried to get everyone else to be convicted. This is a covert way of avoiding personal responsibility for their own issues. One time, I saw a young, immature pastor get up in a leadership meeting and give a ten-minute prophetic diatribe condemning the leaders for their lack of commitment to Jesus. While he was still speaking, one of the older mature leaders got up and gently pushed this young man against the wall while he was crying in the Spirit. The young leader got the message and stopped speaking. Then the leader hosting the meeting explained to the whole group that the young pastor was prophesying out of his own issues regarding areas of his life he was frustrated with.

When you receive a word, whether directly from the Lord or from someone else, it's imperative to discern whether a word is for the church or just for you. The best way forward is to teach people that if they are dealing with anger, guilt, or bitterness, it is probably best they do not operate in the gift of prophecy until they resolve those issues and receive healing from the Lord.

5. Words given to wealthy people

I have noticed that some prophetic people habitually find the wealthiest people in a local church and give them prophecies. Unfortunately, I believe the underlying motivation some have is to make a personal connection with "money people" so they can stay in touch with them and be personally supported. The apostle James condemned showing partiality to the rich as a sin, so be wary of those prophets who gravitate toward the rich.[116]

---

116   James 2:1-10

6. Match-making words

I vividly remember one time in the 1990s when a fifteen-year-old youth came to me during a church service confused after a prophetic leader ministered to him. Since he was newly saved, he was trying to figure out how to fulfill the word he just received, and he desired my advice. He had been told through prophecy that he was going to meet his wife in six months. The one giving him the word must have thought he was a young man in his twenties because he had a full beard! I told the young man that it was a mistake and to forget about the word. I also brought strong correction to the usually accurate prophetic leader and told him never to give words related to marriage again.

Only a few times over the years (thank the Lord!), have I seen prophecies come forth that attempted to connect two people together or paint a vivid picture of what their future spouse will look like. Many will go everywhere trying to match the vivid picture of the prophecy with every person they meet and wonder if this is the person mentioned in the prophecy. Consequently, before a prophetic minister comes to our church, we give them guidelines which include no prophetic words are to be given related to a future spouse or connecting two people together in marriage. By and large, these words are usually not accurate and can cause much consternation, confusion, and hurt for the recipients of the word.

7. Words commissioning people as apostles to nations

In the past few decades, I have seen people being proclaimed as "apostles" to certain cities and or nations. This can damage the recipient of the word, as it can puff them up with pride and presumption. It can damage the Body of Christ in their region, as well. I have heard of people receiving words like this, and it did not lead to good fruit in the Kingdom. After receiving this word, they would attempt to exercise ecclesial authority over pastors and churches. This caused much confusion, division, and resulted in them losing credibility for putting themselves above the other pastors in their nation or city.

Truth be told, in certain complex cities like New York, there are so many people, streams, denominations, and networks (not including the various ethnic networks that do not speak or understand English) that there will usually never be one apostle to a city, but a divergence of apostolic gifts that can contextualize and speak to the needs of the whole city. For example, the church in Jerusalem had twelve apostles, not just one. It's not just presumptuous to assume one will become the sole apostle to a city; it's simply not realistic.

We have to be wary whenever we hear that a person has been declared to be an apostle to a city or nation. Prophetic words like this are often presumptuous and do not usually edify the church in the region.

8. Words assigning a governmental role in the local church

In the late 1980s, a prophetic minister prophesied to our congregation that God was sending me out of the house as a trans-local minister and appointing one of the associate pastors as my successor. Not only was this bad protocol, but it was an inaccurate word! I had to correct this prophetic leader and point out to the church the lack of protocol in this situation.

Since that episode, we now give out guidelines and protocols to visiting ministers instructing them never to appoint a person in our church an elder, or a leader, and or "send them out of the house" without first privately clearing the word with myself or one of our elders. These guidelines have worked well and we have never had another incident like this in over thirty years–even though we still have many prophetic leaders come to the house to minister.

9. Words that point back to the prophet

According to 1 Corinthians 12:3, when the Holy Spirit speaks, He always exalts Jesus as Lord. In other words, the Spirit always points back to Jesus and glorifies God. If a prophetic word comes forth that exalts or praises the speaker or prophet, that is a warning that both the prophetic word and the prophet are out of line and should be shut down.

To discern if the words are pointing back to the prophet, listen very carefully. Prophetic words point back to the prophet when the prophet constantly uses a personal pronoun like "I," or when they say things like, "Hear the voice of the servant of the Lord" while giving the prophecy. All true prophetic words rarely, if ever, refer back to the one giving the prophecy.

10. Words that violate the plain teaching of Scripture

Proverbs 30:5-6 says, "Every word of God is pure; He is a shield to those who put their trust in Him. Do not add to His words, lest He rebuke you, and you be found a liar." I hope it is obvious that any prophetic word that violates one of the cardinal tenets of Scripture should be discarded. So-called prophetic people that preach a different gospel or heretical views related to the Triune God, or that contradict the word of God, should be strongly corrected and in many cases dismissed from ministry until they demonstrate they understand the elementary doctrines of the faith as found in Hebrews 5:12-6:3. If the prophet doesn't affirm the principles of the Bible through their word, they aren't worth listening to.

11. Prophecies given without pastoral oversight and application

I always cringe when I see prophetic gatherings open to the public wherein words are given to believers without their pastor, elder, or a mature leader required to be present to judge the words. Giving words without a mature leader present is dangerous to the one delivering the word and to the one hearing it. Someone can take a word out of context really easily because most people are guilty of selective hearing and will only like certain parts of the word and ignore the corrective aspects of it. 1 Corinthians 14:29 and 1 Thessalonians 5:21 require that every prophetic word be judged in the context of the local church. How can a conference speaker or stranger judge and or apply a word accurately without understanding the life history and context of the individual they give a word to?

12. Self-appointed social media prophets and prophecies

Since this was already dealt with in a previous chapter, I will be brief. With the advent of social media, self-appointed prophets have arisen who frequently give words to cities, nations, and even individuals. Who are these people? Who has vetted their life and ministry? How healthy is their marriage? Who are they accountable to? Unfortunately, charismatic, media-savvy, anointed people can utilize social media to garner a huge platform while bypassing the grid of the local church along with biblical criteria for leadership.[117] If we can't see the kind of fruit they produce, how are we to discern whether they are truly of the Lord?

---

117   1 Tim. 3:1-8

13. When people prophesy beyond their faith and ministry grace

I have witnessed many people who were accurate when it came to dispensing individual prophecies but who missed it big time when they attempted to give prophetic words to cities, regions, and nations. Very few have been able to transition from an individual to a corporate anointing in the prophetic. People make the mistake of thinking that just because they have a grace upon their life to minister to individuals they can eventually graduate to ministering to nations. But this is not always a certainty.

Paul singled out prophecy more than other gifts because of its great ability to edify the church and its usefulness as a tool to train and equip Christ followers.[118] Because of prophecy's unique power, it's important to understand how to discern questionable practices—and questionable people.

118   1 Cor. 14:2, 5

CHAPTER 10

DISCERNING BETWEEN FALSE AND FLAKEY PROPHETS

The prophetic movement has perhaps been one of the most controversial movements in the Body of Christ over the past several decades. Some of it has to do with the fact that many people are afraid of any move of the Spirit, and in their fear, they criticize that which they do not understand. However, I would say that a fair share of criticism against the prophetic is warranted because of either flakey or false prophetic ministries.

When I call a prophet "flakey," I describe a prophetic leader with serious flaws in their ministry, but their heart and motive is generally right before God. I hesitate to call these people truly prophetic people. However, for the sake of the argument, I will leave it as is. When I use the term "false prophet," I am referring to a person who is not only erroneous in their methodology, but in their motive and ambition. This is the kind of person I believe Jesus referred to when He told His followers, "Beware of false prophets, who come to you in sheep's clothing, but inwardly they are ravenous wolves."[119] Frequent patterns of mistakes and or subjectivity can be a sign of a flakey prophet, but a pattern of intentional deceit for self-promotion shows this particular prophetic person to be a false prophet. The former must mature, get mentored, and grow in their prophetic role. The latter has to repent, or they will face the Judgment of God and removal from their ministry.

---

119   Matt. 7:15

SIGNS OF A FLAKEY PROPHET

1. They prophesy ambiguous words.

Their words are so general and ambiguous that it is really hard to tell if it is accurate or not. Consequently, when a supposed prophetic word is too general and open to many interpretations, whether it be a personal prophetic word or national words regarding the church or geo-politics, then it is really not worth pronouncing. In my estimation, those who regularly pronounce this sort of prophetic utterance, even though they may mean well, show signs of flakiness.

2. They prophesy things already stated in the media.

I have read numerous words from so-called prophets that essentially prophesy after the fact—or after it is clear a church or cultural issue or person is trending a certain way. This kind of prophetic word is a waste of time and demonstrates a certain amount of flakiness. Quite frankly, it is tacky and leaves the prophet open to accusations of mimicking natural sources in the name of the prophetic.

3. Their words are so mystical nobody can understand them.

I have been in numerous meetings wherein the prophetic words given were so symbolic and mystical that the congregation or recipient of the words could not understand, nor could they properly apply or interpret them. Thus, when prophetic people don't give practical, applicable words (or teachings) easily understood and interpreted, then their ministry may be flakey.

4. There is no focus or discipline in their ministry and life.

I have observed so-called prophetic people that go around giving generic words who never had enough focus to dig down and build anything substantive. All they do is attend one conference after another or roam from church to church with no tangible fruit regarding the transformation of lives. This, to me, is a sign that they are flakey and need some serious mentoring and spiritual growth.

5. There is no foundational Scripture passage when they preach.

Teaching without a strong foundation on Scripture is flakiness. I have sat under some so-called prophetic people who regularly teach without using any scriptural text as a foundation for their message. Sometimes, if they do base their message on a biblical passage, they never properly expound on the text in their subsequent presentation. Instead, all they do is subjectively share what they feel. While it is good to share what you feel the Lord is saying, the Bible is clear that the word of God equips us, prepares us, and "make[s us] wise unto salvation."[120] Hence, a person who has no word ministry but simply goes about sharing what they feel or sense is not teaching the saints how to apply the Word. They are merely illustrating how people can hear their words, which simply is not enough to build up the Body of Christ.

6. They think every natural and political catastrophe is a sign of the last days.

Every time there is a natural disaster, a war, rumors of war, a financial crisis, or political turmoil, there is somebody either writing an article and or a book about how this fits biblical prophecy and how the end is coming near. However, this is ridiculous. Since the early church, almost every generation has thought that they were the last generation. This generally happens because of a hyper-dispensational interpretation of the passages of Matthew 24, Mark 13, and Luke 21, as well as other books like Revelation, Daniel, and Ezekiel. I and most believers I speak to are sick and tired of these ridiculous "last days" pronouncements. Instead, we take Christ's approach when He told His disciples to focus on the primary mission of the church and not on the "times and the seasons which the Father has put in His own authority."[121] If someone keeps making unfruitful proclamations about the end of days, it's best not to listen to them.

---

120   2 Tim. 3:15-17
121   Acts 1:6-8

7. **They always have extraordinary existential supernatural experiences with no fruit in their ministry.**

I have heard several people telling me that they are always being caught up into heaven, seeing angels, talking with Jesus, the departed saints, and so on. One man even told me I can reserve a trip into heaven to meet Jesus via Facebook! Through the years, I have even had some of these people in our church. Rarely do I see any noticeable, practical fruit in the lives of people like this. They may be so focused on mystical experiences they neglect the practical outworking of their faith.

Now, of course I believe it is possible to be caught up into heaven as Saint Paul was.[122] However, even the apostle Paul did not seem to have these experiences as regularly as some of the believers and prophetic people claim to have them today. I also doubt very much he made an "appointment" with God to have a heavenly trip!

I think it is dangerous when a person says they regularly have conversations with the saints in heaven. This perpetuates the historically erroneous doctrine taught by the Roman Catholic church regarding the practice of praying to the saints and to Mary the mother of Jesus instead of to the Father in the name of Jesus—which is the correct way to pray according to John 14-16.

Although some of the people practicing the things mentioned in this point can also prove to be false prophets, I also think many of these people are merely misguided. They may also have emotional and psychological issues, as well as biochemical imbalances. At best they may be flakey; at worst some may be false prophets. There is some overlap in the traits of flakey prophets and in those of false prophets. However, while flakey prophets usually have their hearts in the right place, false prophets are more intent on leading others astray, and are therefore more dangerous.

THE TRAITS OF FALSE PROPHETS

1. **They prophesy to people based on info they receive on social media.**

I have heard of so-called prophets that will google the names of pastors and people they know they are going to minister to, and then prophesy to

---

122   2 Cor. 12

them things based on specific information already written about them online. Unfortunately, most people are so gullible and so desperate to receive a word from the Lord they will likely not correlate what they wrote online with what they hear from the so-called prophet. Or they will just think it was a confirmation of what they already wrote, sensed, or said about themselves on social media. A person who gathers personal info to prophesy it to others is a false prophet in my book, as they are not seeking the Lord and are attempting to puff themselves up through trickery.

2. They prophesy based on conversations they have had with others.

I had one apostolic prophet visit our church who would spend a long time asking me about specific people in our congregation before he ministered prophetically in our church service. The accurate words he gave were based on the natural information he received in our conversations. The people he attempted to prophesy over without having previous knowledge about them were way off. He did this twice. After the second time I reprimanded him, and he never did this again. Eventually he tried to usurp my authority as the lead pastor, showing his true colors as a false prophet. Again, this dishonesty makes a sham of prophetic ministry.

3. Their staff secretly convey information to them while they prophesy.

I have seen exposés on television regarding phony prophets secretly wearing earpieces so their staff can feed them information about people as they converse with them. Obviously, this intentionally deceptive method of operating in the prophetic demonstrates that this person does not depend upon the Lord to give him supernatural words of knowledge or wisdom, thus exposing himself as a false prophet.

4. They prophesy for financial gain.

False itinerant prophets try to discern who in the congregation has the most money and or are the most vulnerable. Their motive is to endear themselves to these people by giving them a prophetic word, getting their cell phone number, striking up a friendship, and hitting them up for money on a regular basis. I have even heard about some blatant practices in the name of the prophetic who charge money for each prophecy and extra for a "transformational word!" Prophets who operate like this are false prophets since they objectify people and use their gift for financial gain.

5. They put extra-biblical revelation on par with the Bible.

Anyone who insists their "revelation" is equal to Scripture is a false prophet. Not only is this spiritual manipulation, it's also dangerous. The sacred, accepted canon of the sixty-six books of both the Old and New Testament are already settled. God does not take it lightly when we add to His book.[123] When prophetic voices speak like this, they become their own canon and equate their words as equally inspired and important as the sacred Scriptures. Hence, they are already in great error.

Any person who says they have been caught up to heaven and have received additional chapters or books of the Bible to teach is a false prophet. Any person who claims to have a "special revelation" greater than the sacred writings of the prophets and apostles of the Bible are false prophets. Stay away from these people.

6. They point people to themselves.

Scripture teaches us that "the spirit of prophecy" is Christ's testimony, and that if someone is truly inspired by God, they will lift up Jesus as Lord.[124] Contrary to these instructions, false prophets use their gifts to point people to themselves more than to the Lord. As already written in a previous chapter, anyone who promotes, exalts, and points to himself, no matter how accurate their prophetic words are, is either already a false prophet or on the road to becoming one. Such a person needs to repent. They are guilty of promoting idolatry in the church and trying to share the glory of God in a way that displeases Him.[125]

7. They lead people away from biblical orthodoxy.

---

123   Prov. 3:5-6; Rev. 22:18-19
124   Rev. 19:10; 1 Cor. 12:3
125   Is. 42:8

On occasion, I have heard of famous preachers who have said that the Lord showed them things that go outside the bounds of biblical orthodoxy. Several have said that God told them that all people go to heaven whether they believe in Jesus or not. Others have said there are many roads or religions that lead to heaven.

Any preacher or person who says that the Holy Spirit taught them something that clearly disagrees with Scripture is a false prophet.[126] The apostle Paul said, "[E]ven if we, or an angel from heaven, preach any other gospel than what we have preached, let him be accursed."[127]

It is not my desire in this section to cause unnecessary judgment towards others. There may even be new believers who fall into some of the above points out of ignorance. It is my objective to develop discernment in the Body of Christ and to encourage Christ-followers to know the Scriptures and glorify God in everything they participate in. The apostle Paul said, "Imitate me, just as I also imitate Christ."[128] If either I or another spiritual leader doesn't follow Christ in how they act, teach, or live, then do not follow them in that area of their life. May the Lord increase our discernment, and may the Church test the spirits without quenching the Spirit![129]

---

126   Deut. 13:1-4
127   Gal. 1:8-9
128   1 Cor. 11:1
129   1 Thess. 5:19-22

PART III

THE HEALTHY WAY FORWARD FOR PROPHETIC PEOPLE

CHAPTER 11

THE CASE FOR CHRISTIAN MYSTICISM

The American Heritage Dictionary describes mysticism as "a belief in the existence of realities beyond perceptual or intellectual apprehension that are central to being and directly accessible by subjective experience."[130] Paul the Apostle has been my model in ministry for many years because he was both an intellectual who God used as a Christian apologist and also quite a mystic, since he believed God appeared to him and spoke to him regularly—something that would qualify him today as a Christian mystic.

Even though I have degrees in higher Christian learning and have spent more than forty years reading books on theology, church history, apologetics and beyond, I would probably be considered a mystic by some in the Body of Christ because I depend upon hearing the voice of God before I make any major decisions. Unfortunately, many ministers are either intellectually astute and spiritually dry, or illuminated with knowledge from the Spirit but without much sound doctrine. I believe all ministers of the Gospel are called to be both intellectually and spiritually astute; one cannot go without the other. Consequently, the Scriptures should be illuminated by an intense personal communion with the Holy Spirit. Our

---

130   *The American Heritage Dictionary*, s.v. "mysticism," accessed March 26, 2021, https://www.ahdictionary.com/word/search.html?q=mysticism.

illumination and guidance from the Lord should comport with sound doctrine as taught in Scripture.

Many in the Christian fundamentalist camp espouse the doctrine of cessationism, which is the idea that God once spoke to us in His Son, but all subjective communication outside of the Scriptures has ceased, including the revelatory gifts mentioned in 1 Corinthians 12, since "that which is perfect" (which they believe to be the closed and final canon of Scripture) "has come" (Hebrews 1:2; 1 Corinthians 13:9-12).[131]

As a charismatic Bible teacher, I strongly disagree with the cessationist position for personal reasons. The prophetic has been and continues to be incredibly significant in my life. Once, when my son Jason was a freshman in high school, I went on a vacation to Virginia with my wife. A spirit of prayer came upon me for Jason. I sensed that he was in danger and that I had to pray for his protection. I prayed and travailed until I sensed a breakthrough in the spirit and knew he would be ok. Later on, I received a call from my secretary, and she told me that Jason got hit in the head with a hockey stick by another student. She had to rush him to the emergency room for stitches, but thankfully he was okay and there was no permanent damage.

But there are also plenty of theological, historical, and logical reasons why I believe the Lord still speaks through the gifts of the Spirit. To believe in cessationism is to disregard many heroes of the faith, including but not limited to the post-apostolic fathers, St. Augustine, the Desert Fathers, and numerous others who have borne witness to God working through the Spirit. Many of the great revivalists, evangelists, preachers, and great national leaders including Joan of Arc, Catherine of Siena, D.L. Moody, R.A. Torrey, Charles Finney, Charles Spurgeon, John Wesley, George Whitefield, the Moravians, Reformed hero Abraham Kuyper, Maria Woodworth-Etter, Katherine Kulhman, Aimee Semple McPherson, and, in contemporary times, Heidi Baker experienced miracles and/or God speaking to them regarding their ministry.

Nine Reasons Why I Disagree With Cessationism

1. It is not reasonable to teach that the completion of the canon of Scripture brought an end to all miracles and silenced conversations between God and

---

131   Heb. 1:2; 1 Cor. 13:9-12

individuals. I have heard many people say that the canon of Scripture was completed around 70-90 A.D., sometime after John wrote the book of Revelation. However, the full canon of Scripture as we know it today wasn't fully realized until the fourth century, when St. Athanasius compiled all the accepted books of the Bible as part of an Easter letter he wrote to the churches. That being said, even if we consider the canon to be complete in the first century, we know that Christians still saw the Spirit working after that time period. The Didache, a first- and second- century document used to instruct the churches, has guidelines for traveling prophets.[132] Thus, the Church still believed God spoke directly to and through people after the canon of Scripture was technically finished.

Furthermore, this refutes the present day cessationist teaching since the Didache was written anywhere between the end of the first and the end of the second century–likely much later than the final book of the New Testament. Many people believe the book of Revelation was written before the Temple in Jerusalem was destroyed in 70 A.D.[133] Hence, prophets were still recognized long after John the Apostle passed away.

2. Throughout church history, there have always been Christian testimonies of God speaking personally to individuals in the church and performing miracles. Will Graham lists, among others, Irenaeus and Origen, two second-century church fathers, as figures who considered the charismata to be a sign that a believer truly followed the Way.[134] For instance, Irenaeus writes in *Against Heresies*,

> *...those who are in truth Jesus' disciples, receiving grace from him, do in His name perform miracles, so as to promote the welfare of other men, according to the gift which each one has*

132   David Michael Brown, "The Didache and Traditioned Innovation: Shaping Christian Community in the First Century and the Twenty-First Century," (PhD thesis, Divinity School of Duke University, 2016), 94, https://dukespace.lib.duke.edu/dspace/bitstream/handle/10161/12920/Brown_divinity.duke_0066A_10051.pdf?sequence=1&isAllowed=y page 94).

133   Kenneth Gentry, *Before Jerusalem Fell: Dating the Book of Revelation*, Victorious Hope Publishing, 2010.

134   Will Graham, "The Gifts of the Spirit Never Left the Early Church," *Evangelical Focus*, Aeropago Protestante, January 31, 2015, https://evangelicalfocus.com/fresh-breeze/240/the-gifts-of-the-spirit-never-left-the-early-church.

received from Him. For some do certainly and truly drive out devils, so that those who have thus been cleansed from evil spirits frequently both believe in Christ, and join themselves to the Church. Others have foreknowledge of things to come: they see visions, and utter prophetic expressions. Others still heal the sick by laying their hands upon them, and they are made whole. Yea, moreover, as I have said, the dead even have been raised up, and remained among us for many years.[135]

Origen, too, wrote about the presence of the Spirit and its active work in the Body of Christ. In *Against Celsus*, he wrote, "…there are still preserved among Christians traces of that Holy Spirit which appeared in the form of a dove. They expel evil spirits, and perform many cures, and foresee certain events, according to the will of the Logos."[136] From these, and other testimonies from their contemporaries, we see the Spirit clearly moving in the Church. The Spirit didn't stop working in the first century, and He continues working today!

3. To teach that God only speaks through the Scriptures is to take away a large part of His personality and function regarding His relationship with His children. After all, how many people do you know would choose written letters to be the only mode of communication with those they love, like their spouse and children? Writing letters to the people you love is much different from speaking with them face to face. In verbal conversations, you can often see their facial expressions and hear their voices, learning their true feelings as they speak. It builds a different kind of

135 Irenaeus of Lyons, *Against Heresies, in Ante-Nicene Fathers: Vol. 1: The Apostolic Fathers, Justin Martyr, Irenaeus* (Buffalo: Christian Literature Publishing Company, 1885), 2:32:4, retrieved from https://ccel.org/ccel/schaff/anf01/anf01.ix.iii.xxxiii.html, quoted in Will Graham, "The Gifts of the Spirit Never Left the Early Church," *Evangelical Focus*, Aeropago Protestante, January 31, 2015, https://evangelicalfocus.com/fresh-breeze/240/the-gifts-of-the-spirit-never-left-the-early-church.

136 Origen, *Contra Celsus*, in *Ante-Nicene Fathers: Vol. 4: The Writings of the Fathers Down to A.D. 325* (Buffalo: Christian Literature Publishing Company, 1885), 1:46, retrieved from https://www.newadvent.org/fathers/04161.htm, quoted in Will Graham, "The Gifts of the Spirit Never Left the Early Church," Evangelical Focus, Aeropago Protestante, January 31, 2015, https://evangelicalfocus.com/fresh-breeze/240/the-gifts-of-the-spirit-never-left-the-early-church.

intimacy than merely writing to them. Likewise, God wants to build intimacy with us by talking directly to Him, not just reading His Word. Christ told us that His sheep know His voice, and we get to know someone's voice by talking to them.[137]

4. If "perfect" means that God can't speak anymore because the canon of Scripture is complete, then why does David describe the Old Testament as "perfect" (the Hebrew word *tə-mî-māh*) in Psalm 19:7, even before its New Testament counterpart of twenty-seven additional books were added?[138] While *tə-mî-māh* means "entire, whole, complete, perfect, and free from blemishes," *teleó*, the Greek word translated as "perfect" in 1 Corinthians 13:10, has to do with maturity, with being full-grown as opposed to a "babe[ ] in Christ."[139] Hence, this word does not refer to absolute perfection, since it still leaves for more growth as Christ is formed more and more in the person. Saying that the word *teleó* or "perfect" only refers to the Scriptures does not allow for the possible interpretation of the spirits of the just men being made "perfect".[140] In Hebrews 12:23, the word *teleioo*, a linguistic relative of *teleó*, describes those who have attained their final objective or goal. It can also refer to a time when we will all be perfect in heaven after we see Jesus and become like Him.[141]

Paul describes this state of perfection as a time when he would "know just as I also am known".[142] Paul in this passage is speaking about himself, which shows that perfection cannot mean the completion of the canon of Scripture since Paul died before the full canon was completed. Church history tells us that he was beheaded by Nero before the canon was completed by John's writing of the Book of Revelation. Thus, he couldn't have been referring to the completion of the canon of Scripture.[143]

---

137 Jn. 10:27

138 James Strong, *Strong's Hebrew Exhaustive Concordance*, s.v. "tamim," https://biblehub.com/hebrew/strongs_8549.htm; James Strong, *Strong's Greek Concordance*, s.v. "teleo," https://biblehub.com/greek/5055.htm.

139 1 Cor. 3:1-3

140 Heb. 12:23

141 1 John 3:2

142 1 Cor. 13:10, 12

143 Colin Wong, "When Did the Apostle Paul Die?," eBible Questions, eBible.com, May 8, 2013, https://ebible.com/questions/98-when-did-the-apostle-paul-die.

5. I don't know one Christian in all of history who believed they "know just as I also am known" just by reading the Bible.[144] This experience can only be referring to heaven, since even the Scriptures are limited primarily to what we need to understand in this life regarding redemption, which is just a speck of all the knowledge of the Godhead and even human nature and potential. Even if the Scriptures are fully comprehensive regarding God and human nature, we still won't fully understand ourselves until heaven because we are tainted with sin and limited by our flesh.

6. To say that prophecy, tongues, and revelation adds to the word of God and thus are condemned by Scripture does not make sense. Scripture teaches that prophecy should be judged by others in its hearing.[145] It is not adding or taking away from the Scriptures because it is never placed on the same level and authority of Scripture. This would be almost as foolish as saying we should never read or speak about any other book but the Bible because doing so would add or take away from the word of God. What matters is if the person reading other books grants the Bible final authority on all matters regarding lordship and life.

7. To say that all subjective illumination is heretical, adds to the Bible, or the like is not accounting for the fact that the only entity or person that is totally objective is the Godhead. All other things and beings are derivative because they were either made in His image or created by Him. Thus, subjectivity can only be judged by a matter of degrees. For example, when a fundamentalist cessationist believes they are saved because of a witness they have in their spirit, that belief is just as subjective as a prophecy because the witness amounts to God telling them or giving them a sense that they are a child of God. The belief that a person is one of the elect is also subjective and cannot be objectively proven to be true.

Furthermore, what is a word but something that connotes a feeling or a desire? When someone prophesies, they are only articulating with words a sense of something they feel or believe in their heart. So, when someone says that God speaks to them only through Scripture, this means that there must

---

144   1 Cor. 13:12b
145   Rev. 22:18-19; 1 Thess. 5:20-21; 1 Cor. 14:29

be some subjective feeling or interaction in a person's heart that involves more than just ink and paper. The words must be made alive by an illumination or an interactive sense in their spirit or imagination that is extra-biblical. It's the same as when one says, "God laid something on my heart," which is just another way of saying that God spoke to them. Thus, while their nomenclature is different, the subjective experience is not.

8. To deny that God speaks today Spirit-to-spirit or heart-to-heart only through the reading of Scripture is to deny the greatest post-apostolic global movement on the earth, the 1906 explosion of the Pentecostal movement with the Azusa Street Revival. As of 2014, Pentecostalism has almost 300 million adherents worldwide and has easily become the most influential sociological movement since the birth of the church two thousand years ago.[146] Cessationists who teach that Pentecostalism is of the devil must believe that Satan's kingdom is divided against himself since this expression of Christianity is the fastest growing Jesus movement in the Global South!

9. Some might even say they would rather have gifts of healings, miracles, prophecies, and a real experience with the presence, reality, and power of God than the complete canon of Scripture. That is to say, they would rather have a few chapters missing from the books of Leviticus or Revelation and have the miracles than have all the information and no reality, because it is the reality of God that effectively spreads the Gospel.

I personally cannot conceive of a God that couldn't personally speak or move by His power anymore because the last chapter of Revelation was written. Also, what about lands where the full Bible hasn't yet been translated into the native language? Do miracles cease among an illiterate tribe after the translation of the Bible in their tongue is complete? To espouse a view like this is laughable. If Paul, Peter, John, and Jesus depended on miracles, prophecies, and God speaking to them to spread the Gospel, who are we to say that we don't need that same power to confirm God's word and promote His kingdom? Paul, Peter, and John were the writers of Scripture and knew

---

146   David Masci, "Why Has Pentecostalism Grown So Dramatically in Latin America?," Pew Research Center, November 14, 2014, https://www.pewresearch.org/fact-tank/2014/11/14/why-has-pentecostalism-grown-so-dramatically-in-latin-america/.

the Word personally, and Christ Himself is the incarnate Word, yet each still needed the Father to speak to them personally.

As great and as comprehensive as Scripture is, it contains a divine narrative regarding salvation, redemption, and restoration of culture that cannot replace the Holy Spirit's specific guidance and leading. It is one thing to know that Jesus wants me to preach the Gospel and go to the nations, but it is another thing entirely to know which nation He wants me to go to. This can only come from God communicating to our spirits personally regarding His will for our lives.

CHAPTER 12

ARE YOU PURSUING GOD OR A PROPHET?

The prophetic always becomes very popular during a crisis. The uncertainty of our contemporary time motivates people to long for an assuring personal Word from the Lord. Many people who function in the prophetic know they can easily garner many followers on social media by dispensing prophetic statements. However, when we read the Scriptures, we learn that God has called us primarily to know His ways. To know God's ways is to understand His character, attributes, personality, and will. Knowing Him causes a person not only to know His character, but also to know what He loves and loathes.[147] A primary sign that a person fears the Lord is that they love what He loves and hate what He hates.[148] Unlike receiving a prophetic word, understanding God's ways is a lifelong journey.

The best way to get to know God is by continually filling oneself with His Spirit while saturating oneself with the Word of God.[149] One time, a young man asked me for a "word from God." I asked this young man if he went to church. "Rarely," he said. I asked him if he took the time to pray. "Rarely," he said. I asked him if he read his Bible regularly. "Once in a while," he said. I responded, "This is the Word of the Lord for you: Read the Bible and obey it!" Allowing the Word of God to saturate us the same way the rays of the sun saturate the earth will transform us to be like Yahweh.[150] A lifestyle of

147   Ps. 97:10
148   Prov. 8:13
149   Eph. 5:18-20; Ps. 119:97-99
150   Ps. 19

meditating on the Word of God causes us to flourish and bear much fruit because doing so transforms us into His image.[151]

The Bible is filled with references that teach the various attributes of God's character. Consequently, to the extent we know His ways, we can discern His paths.[152] In the early spring of 2020, I was asked to participate on an online panel and give my perspective on the coronavirus. I disagreed with the prophetic voices that indicated it would leave quickly. The reason I disagreed with these statements is not that I had a particular "prophetic word" but because, based on my knowledge of God's ways, I felt this crisis would linger longer than many expected. I discerned that God was presently working through this crisis to purge and prepare His church for a real spiritual awakening.

When we constantly invest our time to get "a word" instead of searching the depths of His character to know Him, we will develop a superficial faith. Prematurely praying for revival without the precondition of "breaking up the fallow ground" is missing the significance of the moment.[153] Scripture admonishes us to earnestly seek Him, to grow in the knowledge of God, and to know Him.

God gets upset when we do not know His ways.[154] Something that set Moses and David apart from others was not only their faith, but their hunger to know and seek God.[155] Moses was able to perform many miracles because He knew God's ways while Israel only observed God's actions.[156] Hence, to the extent that we know God is the extent to which we can make Him known. As a result, we can then express His heart in words that are filled with power, authority, and accuracy. Jesus was able to manifest the fullness of God and make Him known because He was "in the bosom of the Father."[157]

We have to ask ourselves the searing question, "Are we seeking God commensurate to our calling and destiny?" If you aren't, then it should not be a surprise to you as to why you're not maximizing your divine assignment. The

---

151 Ps. 1, 2, 17:15; 2 Cor. 3:8; Rom. 12:1-2
152 Ps. 25:4
153 Hos. 10:12
154 Heb. 3:7-10
155 Ex. 33:13; Ps. 25:4, 42:1-2, 63:1-8, 73:25
156 Deut. 34:10; Ps. 103:7
157 John 1:18, 14:6-11; Heb. 1:1-2

ultimate goal of the gospel is to transform people to maturity and become Christlike, not to go chasing after what we believe our destiny should be.[158]

I believe that during the coronavirus pandemic, God placed the whole world on a forced Sabbath rest. His ultimate goal in all of this is for us to "be still and know that [He] is God."[159] Of course, when in a personal crisis, there is nothing better than receiving an accurate prophetic word from somebody that has no true knowledge of your situation. Unfortunately, the charismatic church is often fixated on the "quick fix" prophetic word instead of a lifetime commitment to know God. A person can receive a transformational prophetic word, but unless it results in that person permanently drawing closer to God, its effect will be short-lived.

According to *The Westminster Shorter Catechism*, man's primary purpose is "to glorify God and to enjoy Him forever."[160] He desires all to "see [His] face in righteousness" and "be satisfied" only by being like Him in the process.[161] May it be so with all believers!

---

158 Rom. 8:29; Eph. 4:13-16; Col. 1:28; 1 Pet. 1:15-16

159 Ps. 46:10

160 *The Westminster Shorter Catechism*, (Edinburgh: The General Assembly of the Church of Scotland, 1648), question 1, accessed April 27, 2021, https://prts.edu/wp-content/uploads/2013/09/Shorter_Catechism.pdf.

161 Ps. 17:15

CHAPTER 13

BECOMING A BIBLICALLY BALANCED PROPHETIC COMMUNITY

Historically, our local church has been dramatically shaped by corporate prophetic ministry. From our inception in 1984, we had rented various facilities and saving up our money for when the opportunity came. But the prices were very high, especially for our youthful church in an at-risk, low income community.

In 1995, my prophetic colleague Jim Jorgenson gave our church a word that we would have our own facility within three years, and I remembered that word. About two and a half years later, during one of our pre-service discipleship meetings, I reminded the men in that group of the word Jim gave. We had only six months to move into our new facility. We began seeking the Lord about it and a mighty spirit of prayer came upon us. Our hearts felt weighed down with a great burden for this need, and we knew it wouldn't let up if we stopped interceding. We knew we were in spiritual warfare and had to keep pushing through in the spirit until we received our breakthrough.

After two hours of struggling in the spirit, we broke through at about noon. Our burden had been replaced with God's peace, and we had a strong sense that God answered our prayer. That afternoon, we had a guest speaker named Floyd Baker for our two p.m. service. When he got up to minister, he called me up to the pulpit before he began to preach. He told me, "The Lord is showing me that you are believing for a building, and that it will come sooner than you think." Floyd had no idea what we were just praying about!

The very next day I was conducting a funeral for Lillian Asman, a faithful long-time member of our church. While I was in the limousine speaking to her son Walter, I asked about the Finnish community in Sunset Park. He told me that the board for a well-known community dance hall voted to sell the property yesterday, and he asked me if I was interested. Of course I was! A few months later, we closed on the property and moved in exactly three years after Jim gave us the prophetic word!

Prophetic ministry can function corporately along with church leadership for the edification of the local church. When I discuss "prophecy" here, I am referring to the simple gift of prophecy mentioned in 1 Corinthians 14:4, which says, "He who speaks in a tongue edifies himself, but he who prophesies edifies the church." I have found that the gift of prophecy is the most faith-building of all the gifts of the Holy Spirit, and I encourage all to prophesy within the boundaries of local church protocol for mutual edification and to develop discernment in the congregation. However, because of its power, it can be the most dangerous gift or the greatest blessing—which is why we need strict guidelines.

Instead of shutting down this gift, we need to properly utilize it with all the biblical checks and balances. We need to ask ourselves these questions:

Am I activated in my prophetic gift? If not, then why not?

Do I understand the importance of the prophetic?

Do I understand how it should operate in the context of my local church?

Paul's Stance

Paul the apostle encouraged the whole Body to prophesy within the framework of the local church. 1 Corinthians 14 says, "Pursue love, and desire spiritual gifts, but especially that you may prophesy... For you can all prophesy one by one, so that all may learn, and all be encouraged."[162]

Despite this clear teaching from Paul, many pastors have functionally shut down the gift of prophecy because of some prophetic extremes and abuses. With this logic, we may as well shut down everything in the church—since every gift and ministry gift has been abused and used in extreme ways. Related to this, Paul said in 1 Thessalonians 5:19–21, "Do not quench the Spirit. Do not despise prophecies. Test all things; hold fast what is good."

---

162   1 Cor. 14:1, 31

Hence, instead of quenching prophecy, we need to have checks and balances, enabling us to test them and validate proper prophetic ministry. That being said, let's explore the best use of this gift in the context of the local church. In this teaching, we are not dealing with prophetic evangelism. Prophetic evangelism has a different set of guidelines, since in evangelism we are not dealing with members of the Body but with those outside of the context of a local church setting.

The five cluster gifts are for the perfecting of the saints for the work of the ministry. Again, we need to understand that Paul always framed all descriptions and functions of the gifts and ministries of the Spirit with the corporate Body of Christ.[163] Jesus said seven times to the seven churches of Revelation to "hear what the Spirit says to the churches."[164] Thus, there are certain things the Lord will not speak to us outside of the context of the local church. These passages can, in principle, also refer to how God will use the gift of prophecy to reveal His will when the congregation is assembled together.

In 1 Corinthians 11, Paul deals with the nature of holy communion, as well as the attitude and proper behavior related to discerning the oneness of the Body of Christ. After this profound teaching on holy communion and corporate unity, chapter 12 teaches on the gifts in the context of the oneness of the church as the Body of Christ. In 1 Corinthians 12:4-8, the manifestations of the Spirit were given in the context of the Body of Christ. Prophecy is mentioned in this passage as one of the nine manifestations of the Spirit given for the edification of the local church. 1 Corinthians 12:12-13 says, "For as the body is one and has many members, but all the members of the body, being many, are one body, so also is Christ. For by one Spirit we were all baptized into one body—whether Jews or Greeks, whether slaves or free—and all have been made to drink into one Spirit." In light of this passage, it is not a coincidence that the teaching on the gifts of the Holy Spirit is given in the context of the corporate nature of the Body of Christ. This, of course, goes against the individualism that is rampant in the contemporary church—especially regarding rogue prophetic ministries that claim to give the word of the Lord on social media without any accountability!

---

163   Rom. 12:3-8; Eph. 4:11-12
164   Rev. 3:22

The True Motivation of the Holy Spirit

Scripture makes it clear that the Holy Spirit always points to Jesus. Hence, all His manifestations should do the same. In John 15:26, Jesus said that the Spirit was sent to glorify and bear witness of Him. "But when the Helper comes, whom I shall send to you from the Father, the Spirit of truth who proceeds from the Father, He will testify of Me." In 1 Corinthians 12:3, Paul says, "Therefore I make it known to you that no one speaking by the Spirit of God calls Jesus accursed, and no one can say that Jesus is Lord except by the Holy Spirit." Paul said this in the context of the false gifts of prophecy given by the "pagan oracles" who worshipped idols and devils, as we see in 12:1-2. Consequently, when the Spirit is truly moving through someone to prophesy, the ensuing Spirit-induced exhortation should point to the lordship of Jesus Christ, as well as motivating all to worship Him. John the Revelator said in Revelation 19:10c, "For the testimony of prophecy is the spirit of Jesus." Consequently, if the prophetic word points to the prophet giving the word instead of to Jesus, its motivation is of the flesh or is demonic in nature.

The Corporate (Body) Nature of Prophecy

Paul continues his teaching on the nature and administration of the manifestations of the Spirit. 1 Corinthians 12:5-7 says, "There are differences of ministries, but the same Lord. And there are diversities of activities, but it is the same God who works all in all. But the manifestation of the Spirit is given to each one for the profit of all." This passage teaches that all the gifts of the Spirit—including prophecy—are given for the common good. Thus, as previously noted, we should conclude that there is really no such thing as "personal prophecy," since all true prophecy should lead to the common good and edification for the whole body. Even prophetic words given to an individual should be connected to calling to advance and edify the Body of Christ for the sake of His Kingdom.

Based on this clear teaching of this passage, as well as the rest of the New Testament, we have to conclude that nobody can fulfill their calling in Christ apart from being a functional member of the Body of Christ as expressed in the local church. Paul writes in 1 Corinthians 12:14-18,

> *For the body is one member but of many. If the foot should say, 'Because I am not a hand, I am not of the body,' is it therefore not of the body? And if the ear should say, 'Because I am not*

> *an eye, I am not of the body,' is it therefore not of the body. If the whole body were an eye, where would be the hearing? If the whole body were an ear, where would be the smelling? But now God has set the members, each one of them, just as He pleased.*

Just as each part of the human body is important and necessary for proper functioning, so is each part of the Body of Christ.

Furthermore, to make sure there is no manipulation and or abuse in regard to the use of the gifts, Paul teaches in the context of his description of the gifts that the vessel carrying said gifts has to do it in love.[165] In 1 Corinthians 13:1–6, Paul says,

> *Though I speak with the tongues of men and of angels, but have not love, I have become sounding brass or a clanging cymbal. And if I have the gift of prophecy, and understand all myster-ies and all knowledge, and though I have all faith, so that I could remove mountains, but have not love, I am nothing. And though I bestow all my goods to feed the poor, and though I give my body to be burned, but have not love, it profits me nothing. Love suffers long and is kind; love does not envy; love does not parade itself, is not puffed up; does not behave rudely, does not seek its own, is not provoked, thinks no evil; does not rejoice in evil, but rejoices in the truth...*

In light of the love passage above, we need to examine the motivation, words, and actions of those giving prophetic words. If they are pointing to or lifting up themselves, boasting, propping up their authority, or acting in a rude, inconsiderate manner, then there is a good chance the word is manipulative and not from the heart of God.

The Corporate Function of the Gift of Prophecy

In chapter 14, Paul gives practical instructions related to its proper use of prophecy in the corporate setting. Here, Paul singles out prophecy as the highest gift to pursue because of its power to edify the church. 1 Corinthians 14:2-5 says,

---

165   1 Cor. 12, 14

For he who speaks in a tongue speaks not to men but to God; for no one understands him; however, in the spirit he speaks mysteries. But he who prophesies speaks edification and exhortation and comfort to men. He who speaks in a tongue edifies himself, but the one who prophesies edifies the church. I wish you all spoke with tongues, but even more that you prophesied; for he who prophesies is greater than he who speaks in tongues, unless indeed he interprets, that the church may receive edification.

In verse 2, Paul describes the private gift of speaking in tongues—which is to aid you as your personal prayer language. This does not refer to utilizing the gift of languages to minister prophetically to others, in which case you would need to interpret your languages for the Church to be edified.[166]

Verse 3 describes the function of the simple gift of prophecy: edification, exhortation, and comfort. Notice nothing is said here about the gift of prophecy being used for general guidance. It is dangerous to be led solely by the prophetic words of others. Furthermore, every word should confirm what God has already said to you. Prophecy should not take the place of the sons of God being led by the Spirit of God.[167] Prophetic words also have to line up with the teaching of Scripture—which includes getting pastoral council from your spiritual leaders.[168] As we will see later on, all prophecies should be done in the context of the local gathering so other spiritual leaders can judge the word.

The Corporate Protocol for the Gift of Prophecy

In 1 Corinthians 14:23-25, Paul says,

Therefore if the whole church comes together in one place, and all speak in tongues, and there come in those who are uninformed or unbelievers, will they not say that you are out of your mind? But if all prophesy, and an unbeliever or uninformed person comes in, he is convinced by all, he is convicted by all. And thus the secrets of his heart are revealed; and so, falling

---

166   1 Cor. 14:5
167   Rom. 8:14
168   Heb. 13:7

down on his face, he will worship God and report that God is truly among you.

This shows that the power of prophecy is effective even for unbelievers—not just believers. Through prophecy, an unbeliever can see the power of God.

Verses 26-28 say, "How is it then, brethren? Whenever you come together, each of you has a psalm, has a teaching, has a tongue, has a revelation, has an interpretation. Let all things be done for edification. If anyone speaks in a tongue, let there be two or at the most three, each in turn, and let one interpret. But if there is no interpreter, let him keep silent in church and let him speak to himself and to God." These guidelines were given so we don't scare new people and or interrupt the flow of the church meeting. Thus, we are to speak in tongues quietly to ourselves unless we believe it is an anointed tongue meant for someone to interpret it. In that case, it functions in the same manner as a prophecy.

Paul continues in verse 29, "Let two or three prophets speak, and let the others judge." Paul seems to limit the amount of people giving prophetic words in a church gathering to two or three people. This limitation may be in place to bring order and focus to the service. I have been in services where more than a dozen people gave prophetic words. After a while, there was chaos and a loss of order and direction. Two to three prophets is sufficient for a service.

This section also shows the importance of giving and receiving prophetic words in the presence of other spiritual leaders and mature saints so the words can be properly judged. This is to protect both the one giving the prophecy, so their words are interpreted and directed properly, as well as the one receiving the prophetic word so mature leaders can help them discern and apply it.

Verses 30-33 say, "But if anything is revealed to another who sits by, let the first keep silent. For you can all prophesy one by one, that all may learn and all may be encouraged. And the spirits of the prophets are subject to the prophets. For God is not the author of confusion but of peace, as in all the churches of the saints." This important passage demystifies the flow of the prophetic, showing that the Holy Spirit doesn't force anyone to give a prophetic word. Even when someone is prophesying, they are in control over their own emotions, will, and actions. Consequently, there is never an excuse for a person giving a prophetic word that interrupts the flow of the service, as the inevitable confusion from such an interruption would not reflect God's nature at all.

To build a biblically balanced prophetic community, we have to ask ourselves the following questions:

- Do you earnestly desire to move in the prophetic gifts? If not, then why not? (Don't you desire to build up the Body of Christ, as well as expose the secrets of the hearts of the non-believer?)

- If you do desire the prophetic gifts, is your motivation to prophesy to glorify Jesus or gain attention for yourself and manipulate others?

- Will you allow God to activate your prophetic gifts today?

- Are there solid prophetic people in your church who can walk with you to develop this gift inside of you?

May the Lord raise up a powerful, prophetic company of believers that will glorify Jesus and manifest His Kingdom.

CHAPTER 14

DEVELOPING A PROPHETIC CULTURE IN YOUR CHURCH

A prophetic culture is an exciting and much-needed element for a cutting-edge local church. By "prophetic culture," I am referring to having a sense of anticipation among the attendees that God is going to manifest His presence and speak directly to His people, either through the preached Word of God or through the worship experience, not just a plethora of prophetic words released during church services. When a church has a true prophetic culture, there is a deep connection to God during congregational gatherings, resulting in believers getting transformed and consecrating themselves to the call of God. When there are many prophetic words but no personal transformation, folks are mainly prophesying out of their own souls and not representing God's heart. There are several things needed to bring a genuine prophetic atmosphere into a local church.

Minister to the Lord instead of entertaining men.

Often when I observe local church worship services, it has more of a performance orientation then a worship orientation. When the focus is on performance, the goal is to entertain the attendees rather than minister to the Lord. Ministering to the Lord is much different from merely attempting to drum up enthusiasm and hype up the people emotionally. A church that learns to minister to the Lord will also have regular seasons of God speaking corporately to their local church regarding their destiny and calling. This will release a powerful prophetic culture in the congregation.

Have regular seasons of congregational fasting and prayer.

Our local church has had a weekly prayer meeting for over thirty years, and we have seen Him work mightily through it. It is often during these meetings that God has spoken to the leaders and me about what He is saying and doing during that season of our church life. Furthermore, we have set aside three times per year when we consecrate days for corporate fasting and prayer. During these times people are empowered, lives are changed, and the church experiences a time of cleansing and repentance. A church that doesn't have regular, vibrant prayer is not allowing God to speak clearly and drill down deep to get at the root issues of sin and lethargy. Churches like this may have a great organizational flow and many good programs, but lives are not being transformed and discipleship stagnates. Like Samson of old, many churches like this would not even know it if the Holy Spirit left them.

Exhort the elders and worship team to seek God.

Leaders who do not live to seek God will not be able to lead the church into their prophetic destiny. Leadership not surrendered fully to living in the presence of God is left concocting mere strategies and programs that leave their congregation empty and powerless. Only leaders who seek God can usher in a prophetic culture.

Many musicians and singers I have met in the Body of Christ have no personal prayer life. They are committed to the church only because it gives them a platform to express their skill. Only worship leaders and musicians that seek God as a team and in private can be sensitive enough to usher in a prophetic culture in their congregation.

Let the gift of prophecy function amongst the members.

The Apostle Paul tells us in 1 Cor. 14:1 to earnestly desire spiritual gifts, especially prophecy. Prophecy is the greatest gift when it comes to edifying the church according to Paul the apostle. Prophecy can come forth through the anointed and authoritative preached word or it can be an anointed exhortation expressing the heart of God from any believer present in the congregation. 1 Corinthians 14 gives rules for the use of this powerful gift so everything is done decently and in an orderly fashion, but in the name of biblical order many churches have shut down this gift totally. One of the greatest ways to create a prophetic culture in the church is to encourage use of this gift with biblical guidelines every time believers come together.

To cultivate this gift in your services, you need to find out what works best for your congregation. Our local church primarily practices this gift in small groups or during altar calls when people are being prayed for. We generally have too many people during our Sunday services for a prophetic exhortation to be heard from a person without a microphone. If someone believes they have a word of the Lord for the church, they have to write it down and submit it to one of the pastors leading the service who will discern whether or not it should be read to the congregation. In large congregational gatherings, it is difficult for non-leaders to use this gift corporately, and when it is used to minister to another individual, there should always be a designated leader present to judge the word.

Equip the congregation to commune with God.

God has given the church many doors to enter His manifest presence, but the most common way is through prayer. Many believers understand just one kind of prayer, usually intercession or petition. This is greatly limiting, since there are many other expressions of prayer. The greatest way to equip the Church to commune with God is to observe how spiritually mature leaders seek God during corporate prayer gatherings. Learning how to pray and seek God is better caught than taught. Believers can learn from mature God-seekers the various movements of how God draws us into His presence and orchestrates corporate seeking. However, for the prophetic culture to permeate the church there should also be congregational instruction.

Instruction should include topics such as waiting upon the Lord, the difference between worship and praise, meditation upon the word of God, intercession, supplication, spiritual warfare, and the prayer of faith. The better-versed a church is regarding these various ways of interacting with the Father, the more the prophetic culture will permeate that church.

Preach the word of the Lord every week.

The lead pastor should be a voice for the Lord and not merely an echo of men. Too many pastors are too busy to seek God. The result is they often retrieve their sermons online or from commentaries. (These commentaries are good tools to inform a sermon but should not be mimicked in its entirety.)

When a lead pastor is primarily a God seeker, they will not only study and pray to prepare sermons, but will teach out of the overflow of their robust private devotional life. Perhaps nothing creates a prophetic culture in a local church more than when people know they are going to hear what the Spirit is saying to their church through the preached word every Sunday.

Along with a prophetic culture, it is vital that the Body of Christ embrace all of the five cluster gifts mentioned in Ephesians 4:11. If only the prophetic is embraced and celebrated, it will throw a church out of balance. It takes all five expressions of the ministry DNA of Jesus to fully mature the saints. May the Lord develop a prophetic culture in every true church in the world so we can impact our communities. After all, it is "not by might or by power but by [His] Spirit,' says the Lord..."[169]

---

169   Zech. 4:6

CHAPTER 15

EMBRACING THE APEST CULTURE IN YOUR LOCAL CHURCH

Although this book is about the prophetic, there cannot be a mature expression of this ministry gift without the counterbalance of the other four gifts in the APEST cluster. APEST is an acronym for the spiritual gifts of Ephesians 4:11: apostle, prophet, evangelist, shepherd (or pastor), and teacher. As a matter of fact, one of the primary reasons some in the prophetic have gone out of whack in the past decade is because they have isolated themselves from the other four gifts. The church needs evangelists to spread the good news, apostles for governance and accountability, teachers for correct biblical exegesis and methodological praxis, and pastors for the proper protocols necessary to protect and care for believers who follow their ministry. These gifts give the Church a balanced menu in a believer's spiritual diet.

In the context of our particular local church, we have developed all APEST ministry functions in our leadership and have historically utilized these expressions in our preaching team. My apostolic message gets regularly balanced out by prophetic, pastoral, teaching, and evangelistic voices in the context of our pulpit and church ministry, presenting our congregation with a balanced menu for their spiritual diet. Both our local church and the Christ Covenant Coalition, (or CCC) have been walking out APEST in a way that we have tried to align with the way of Christ and His apostles as illustrated in the Book of Acts and the Pauline epistles. In the CCC, the private apostolic network I oversee, we all use our gifts to minister to the whole body. When I can't be at my local church, other pastors will step in to preach for me, and we fill in for each other when emergencies arise. Our regular leadership tables also have a robust dialogical format which edifies us collectively as we share insights in Scripture.

In general, embracing the Ephesians 4:11 APEST culture has made huge strides in the overall Church since the mid-20th century. Many in the Church are seeing the need for their churches, movements, and leaders to adopt an apostolic paradigm for the sake of missional expansion. But, as they are new to these ideas, many use the terms and titles without the proper function, resulting in no biblical fruit. Titles should never be the focus of the APEST gifts; the focus should be using those gifts to glorify God and edify the Body. Just because somebody calls themselves an "Apostle" doesn't mean they have apostolic fruit. As a matter of fact, most of the genuine apostles I know rarely call themselves apostles. (One important caveat regarding the title of "apostle": There will never be another group of foundational "apostles of the Lamb" like the original twelve Jesus chose.[170] All other apostles are apostles with a small "a" not a capital "A" like the ones Jesus chose in the gospels.[171])

To understand the role of APEST in maturing the saints, we need to examine Ephesians chapter 4, which has been called by some the architectural centerpiece of the house of God. God calls people with unique ministry gifts to lead His church, and we need to look at the proper framework qualifying how the Body should function together in attitude and character.[172] The following thoughts are related to understanding the strengths of your local church by understanding the particular ministry gift function of the visionary pastor. Because of the nature of this chapter, I am limiting the definitions of "ministry gifts" to the ecclesiastic realm of the kingdom of God.

As we move forward, there are some key questions to ask yourself:

- Do I know which APEST gift I am called to flow in?

- Do I know the primary objective for a Christ follower?

---

170   Rev. 21:14

171   Mark 3:13-14

172   Eph. 4:11

- Am I endeavoring to work in sync with the corporate son or merely as an individual achiever?

Maturing as Sons through APEST

> *I, therefore, the prisoner of the Lord, beseech you to walk worthy of the calling with which you were called, with all lowliness and gentleness, with longsuffering, bearing with one another in love...*[173]

Paul's objective here is to explicate how the church should walk in the character and ministry of Jesus so they can emerge as mature sons committed to the mission of Jesus in this world. Understanding this chapter unlocks the destiny of the church as sons of God.

Before Paul teaches on the APEST ministry gifts, he grounds them in the character of Christ. It is never good for the Church when believers strive only to mimic the ministry of Jesus while neglecting the character of Jesus. Our ministerial platform will only be as effective in proportion to the depth of the knowledge and character of Jesus worked inside of our life. Scripture illustrates that our character is the foundation of the rest of our life, especially in places like the book of Proverbs, the Sermon on the Mount, as well as the history of the Kings of Israel. We are never to build our life upon our gifts and abilities. Our primary focus should be knowing God and giving Him space to operate inside us so the character and person of "Christ is formed in of us."[174]

In Ephesians 4:3, Paul mentions that, in our calling, we must be "endeavoring to keep the unity of the Spirit in the bond of peace." Hence, the APEST leader should have a heart for the corporate calling, destiny, and unity of the faith in the church. A Lone Ranger who is only concerned about building their own empire is in danger of being an immature leader whose ministry platform exceeds the foundation of their character.

Verses 4-6 speak to the importance of unity in the Church. Paul tells the Ephesians that they belong to "one body and one Spirit," and that they share "one Lord, one faith, one baptism; one God and Father of all, who is above all, and through all, and in you all." This passage also illustrates that APEST

173   Eph. 4:1-2
174   2 Pet. 3:18; Gal. 4:19

leaders should be grounded in the key doctrines and first principles of the faith that was "once for all delivered to the saints.[175] They all hold to the same faith.

They also understand that there is only one baptism. Baptism is in this context is connected to being accepted to the life of Christ's Church, again emphasizing the corporate reality of APEST function.

The Ministry Gifts

Verses 7-8 continue, "But to each one of us grace was given according to the measure of Christ's gift. Therefore He says, 'When He ascended on high, He led captivity captive, and gave gifts to men.'"[176] This seems to indicate that every person in the church has been granted at least one of the APEST gifts. At least one of the APEST expressions has been bestowed upon each believer. Furthermore, the fact that verse 8 frames the context illustrates that Paul identified APEST with "Christ's gift." Christ the Messiah is the exemplar demonstration of the fullness of each of the APEST functions in the four Gospels. Jesus is our apostle, prophet, evangelist, teacher, shepherd.[177] Hence, the five cluster gifts are the ministerial DNA of Jesus Himself.

The implications of this are startling. We need to recognize how the ministry DNA of Jesus functions in both the workplace and the church place. Thus, it is not only for those called into full-time church ministry, but for all within the Church.

Paul continues with an exposition of Christ's mission post-crucifixion: "(Now this, 'He ascended'—what does it mean but that He also first descended into the lower parts of the earth? He who descended is also the One who ascended far above all the heavens, that He might fill all things.)"[178] Christ's purpose in ascending, according to verse 10, is to "fill all things," not merely church buildings which alludes to His ultimate Kingdom goal of uniting all things—both things visible and invisible in the heavens and the earth—under the Lordship of Christ.[179] APEST has implications for how every realm in society can be impacted by the reign of Jesus, as we will see in verse 12.

---

175   Jude 3.
176   Eph. 4:7-8
177   Heb. 3:1; Heb. 1:1-2; Luke 4:18; John 3:1-2; John 10:1-30
178   Eph 4:9
179   Col. 1:15-20

Paul then lays out the purpose of the APEST gifts. He continues, "And He Himself gave some to be apostles, some prophets, some evangelists, and some pastors and teachers, for the equipping of the saints for the work of ministry, for the edifying of the body of Christ."[180] The primary purpose of the redeemed APEST gift is to equip or place the holy ones properly in the context of the Body of Christ. Therefore, APEST expressions in the workplace and the Church are called equally to equip one another according to the measures of the gift of Christ and their placement in the Church.

Since Jesus created the world, His ministry DNA is in every human because we are made in His image. Hence, APEST is evident even before a person is saved. After salvation, God redeems the APEST gift inside of each person and utilizes it and anoints it and guides it for His Kingdom. Remember, the context as shown in 4:10 is that Jesus ascended to fill all things, not just church buildings! This means the APEST gifts are called to function in every realm of society. The Church has to rethink its role in regard to preparing plumbers, not just pastors, for their Jesus-centric missional role in the workplace.

We can see the gifts of APEST everywhere. Apostles in the Church and workplace are the pioneers, the entrepreneurs, those who can multiply businesses and create a franchise. This is why Jesus started His movement by appointing twelve apostles, not twelve teachers, prophets, evangelists or shepherds. He needed people with a missional call that were not risk-averse, good with spontaneous problem-solving, liminality, and expansion. Apostles are good at starting churches and getting different ministries off the ground. Ray Kroc is an excellent example of how an apostle would work in the contemporary workplace. He took Richard and Maurice McDonald's restaurant from being a local establishment and grew it into a huge worldwide franchise.[181]

Prophets are those who understand trends, the futurists in both the Church and the marketplace. They see beyond the here and now and share what they see with the Church to encourage fellow believers or warn them of potential spiritual danger. A prophet in the secular world would be able to predict future trends and thought in culture, science, and economics.

---

180 Eph. 4:11-12

181 *Encyclopedia Britannica Online*, s.v. "Ray Kroc," last modified January 10, 2021, https://www.britannica.com/biography/Ray-Kroc.

Some futurists in the past predicted the internet; modern technology, as well as many of the current challenges in the world. Some well-known futurist writers include H.G. Wells, Alvin and Heidi Toffler, Buckminster Fuller, and Ray Bradbury. Evangelists are the influencers, those great in sales, marketing, and promotions who can garner huge crowds and followers in the Church and workplace. These skills attract people, thus furthering the spread of the Gospel.

Teachers are those who can take complex ideas and structures and break them down to a simple user-friendly manual for all to follow. They can explain doctrinal and theological concepts without overwhelming their audience. Public schoolteachers or those called to the education sphere in both the Church and in the workplace have these gifts. Some historically great teachers include the philosophers Aristotle and Pythagoras and scientists like Isaac Newton and Albert Einstein. Shepherds are those involved in care ministry like nurses, counselors, psychologists, or pastors in local churches. They exhibit the compassion of the Father in their work, inviting others into the family of God.

Of course, even though every believer has received this ministry grace, not everyone is called to be a spiritual leader or authority in the church.[182] Only some are uniquely qualified and gifted to oversee the local church with the capacity to affect all the participating workplace and church place members.

The APEST Goal

Paul mentions that our gifts are to encourage the Church and minister to others.

> ...till we all come to the unity of the faith and of the knowledge of the Son of God, to a perfect man, to the measure of the stature of the fullness of Christ; that we should no longer be children, tossed to and fro and carried about with every wind of doctrine, by the trickery of men, in the cunning craftiness of deceitful plotting, but, speaking the truth in love, may grow up in all things into Him who is the head—Christ...[183]

---

182   Eph. 4:7
183   Eph. 4:13-15

"Perfect man" here means "mature," and as the whole Church collectively matures, we manifest the fullness of Christ to the world. This tells us that we still need the APEST functioning because the Body of Christ has not yet reached the unity of the faith and to the maturity of the fullness of Christ. This also aligns with what Paul said in Colossians, the sister epistle of Ephesians: "Him we preach, warning every man and teaching every man in all wisdom, that we may present every man perfect in Christ Jesus. To this end I also labor, striving according to His working which works in me mightily."[184]

In verse 14, Paul describes spiritual children as ones easily swayed by falsehoods.[185] They don't understand the first principles of the faith and are vulnerable to false doctrine.[186] Unfortunately, as we have witnessed in the recent prophetic/charismatic crisis, many pastors lack biblical depth and are tossed to and fro based on the latest popular trends and prophetic words released on the internet. The trickery of men can apply to the biased narratives espoused today in the popular media and those easily led astray by groupthink. Many leaders also put their ethnicity and political party ahead of Kingdom principles, and still others are given to gossip and slander and posture themselves up into the pecking order of the Church or denomination. These are all signs of immature children who have not yet grown into mature manhood in Christ.

Consequently, the goal of APEST is to mature the Church so it collectively functions as a corporate son. This is a significant assignment since the Church is the called the Body of Christ, which means it is the visible manifestation of the invisible Son of God.[187] However, the maturity of the sons of God in a local church is not illustrated by how gifted the lead pastor is. It is instead illustrated by how many people love, serve, and edify one another and are also released to the work of the ministry in the Church and the workplace. In verse 16, Paul says, "...from whom the whole body, joined and knit together by what every joint supplies, according to the effective working by which every part does its share, causes growth of the body for the edifying of itself in love."[188] Paul is saying that each part of the Body works

---

184 Col. 1:28-29
185 Eph. 4:14
186 Heb. 5:12
187 Col. 1:15
188 Eph. 4:1

together to build up the Church. A healthy Body is one where all the parts function properly, and when everyone in the Church does his or her part, the whole Body gets stronger.

Now let's do a deeper dive and explicate each of the APEST functions and see how each ministry gift affects the culture of a local church. Please note: the following is meant to a broad-brush summary that describes APEST churches in their raw, immature state. Those that mature will have more balance than what is illustrated in the following section.

APEST CHURCH MINISTRY GIFTS

Apostle:

In the context of the local church, this person walks in and out of all the ministry gift functions according to the need. Generally, these are God's generals in the Body of Christ who function as leaders over other ministry gift leaders in both the local and regional church. Apostolic leaders plant churches; some oversee a very strong apostolic church that reproduces and sends out other ministry gifts. (See the churches of Jerusalem and Antioch in the book of Acts.) Many oversee a network of other pastors and churches with influence in their region. Some may lead smaller churches, but have very strong congregations with holistic ministries serving their local community. They should also have faith for miracles, especially in the areas of finances and kingdom expansion. They should walk in great wisdom from God based on knowing His ways intimately. Hence, they should frequently move in the gifts of the Spirit with a redemptive gift of leadership.[189] They should have thick skin and walk in unconditional love with much patience in affliction.[190] They are often either great administrators or great managers who are able to oversee large organizations with numerous employees and big budgets. They are also great visionary leaders on the cutting edge of what God wants to do to reach their community and beyond.

Since "apostle" doesn't describe a specific mode of ministry delivery like the other ministry gifts, they usually function strongly in one or two of the other four ministry gifts depending on which ministry gift they operated in

189   1 Cor. 12; Rom. 12:8
190   2 Cor. 11:17-33

prior to becoming apostolic. In my case, I started off in the ministry as an evangelist/prophet. Now, the teaching gift motivated by the prophetic is the strongest anointing that presently flows out of me.

Prophet:

With the apostle, prophets serve as a foundational gift for all other ministry gifts and for the Body of Christ.[191] They are usually endowed with the gift of exhortation. Hence, many are great preachers with great insights from the Lord.

Consequently, apostolic and prophetic leaders differ in these ways. What an apostle speaks from principle, a prophet prophesies from the heart of God. Prophets are also often great visionary leaders with much insight and foresight regarding future trends for the Church and the culture. Their insight also applies to the true condition of the Body of Christ in their region. Prophetic leaders also regularly move in the revelatory gifts of prophecy, discerning of spirits, and interpretation of tongues.

In light of the above, a true, seasoned New Testament prophet can serve as a senior pastor, oversee an apostolic network, or serve as an elder in a local church. Thus, it is hard to tell the difference between apostolic and prophetic leadership. Other prophetic traits may include a strong sense of right and wrong with a tendency to see the world in black-and-white instead of gray, like the shepherd. Many are introverts who desire a lot of time alone with God. They usually have a deep prayer life, often live a solitary life without a broad and active social life, and would rather be with God than men.

Evangelist:

New Testament evangelists regularly move in signs and wonders to confirm the Gospel to unbelievers.[192] They are usually compelling communicators who can break down the Gospel into simple stories that produce great faith for salvation, deliverance, healing, and commitment to fulfill the Great Commission.[193] They are motivated by a great burden for the lost and for outreach. They have an anointing for gathering with great power to influ-

---

191   1 Cor. 12:28
192   Acts 8:1-8
193   Matt. 28:19-20

ence masses of people. Many of the world's largest megachurches are led by evangelist/shepherds.

Shepherd (Pastor):

Shepherds (commonly called "pastors") function with a strong anointing in compassion, mercy, grace, and nurturing to care for the sheep. Hence, they are more concerned with in-reach than outreach. They are also more concerned with relational activities than evangelistic activities. In the church, they focus more on quality than quantity. They love being with people and are motivated by love more than managing programs, and enacting strategies to bring in crowds. Thus, shepherds usually have in their repertoire a ministry that includes counseling, consoling, and comforting the sheep.

Teacher:

Those operating in this ministry DNA have a didactic, systematic mind and approach to everything. They are often introverts who are highly detail-oriented with gifts in administration and management. Bible teachers especially should exhibit a deep yearning to study the word of God and should consider some form of systematic, ordered learning to gain more biblical competency.

Lead pastors functioning in this APEST gift usually prefer to conduct a series of practical and informational messages for their congregation on Sundays instead of disconnected motivational messages. They usually like to feed the flock "the meat of the word" rather than simplistic evangelistic messages. APEST teachers expound the Word with great authority and anointing without having to raise their voice. They usually greatly desire to disciple members in the church, often with some sort of formal approach to teaching such as setting up a Bible school or classes. Their highest ideal is to have a church rooted and grounded in the word and doctrine.

The Corporate APEST Culture in Local Churches

The Scriptures teach that all life reproduces after their own kind.[194] Furthermore, the Scriptures teach that the one sent is never greater than the one

---

194   Gen. 1:11-28; 2 Kings 2:9-15

who sent him.[195] Since this law of impartation and reproduction is true for all living things, APEST is no exception. It should reproduce and impart gifts to members of the Body of Christ according to their ministry grace based on their spheres of influence—including their local church. We see how the spirit of Moses came upon the seventy elders of Israel so they could help bear his burden of leadership.[196] Along those lines, Matthew 10:41 teaches us that the prophet's reward is the prophetic deposit from the prophet that comes to those that receive his ministry. Hence, the local church will take upon itself the culture, anointing, and characteristics of the APEST function of their senior leader and visionary.

In light of all this, we can deduce that if the senior leader is an apostle, the church will be an apostolic church. If the senior leader is a pastor, the church will become a pastoral church, etc. However, while one gift may take precedence under senior leadership, it is crucial for all five APEST ministry gifts to work together in the context of the local church. When all these gifts work together, there is much less room for unbalanced teaching and misuse of the gifts of the Spirit.

Characteristics, Strengths, and Needs of Each APEST Ministry Characteristic

From my observation, congregations led by apostolic leaders will usually have strong administration with many good systems flowing. The church will often operate with strong principles and protocol for leadership, programs, and ministerial processes.

The apostolic church that functions according to the Pauline tradition will reproduce numerous leaders who will be sent out and function either as apostles or as one of the other APEST gifts. The church should also have strong regional influence, either because of its size or because of its holistic ministry and compassionate organizations.

Although apostolic churches are strong, they also have blind spots and weaknesses that will be counterbalanced by partnering with other APEST churches and leaders. Apostles are highly principled people, but they need to be motivated to flesh them out for the world. Apostolic churches often need to have prophets and evangelists regularly visit to inspire the church and

---

195   John 13:16
196   Num. 11:24-25

balance the emphasis on the principled approach as opposed to the motivational approach.

Apostles also tend to overlook the relational aspects of their church, as they concentrate on the work of propagating the gospel and organizational development. Apostolic churches also need to raise up a strong pastoral care ministry to balance this tendency, as well as evangelists to build bridges to other churches and ministries needed to fulfill the Great Commission.

Many high-capacity apostolic leaders are tempted to merely build their own empires instead of advancing His kingdom. Therefore, apostolic churches often need prophetic ministry to remind the apostolic church to regard the needs of the whole kingdom, not just their own Kingdom assignment.

Prophetic churches are often known to cultivate much prayer and intercession along with much fasting for the will of God to be done in the nation. They usually have strong worship and preaching services coupled with the promulgation of great vision. They consistently have unique, insightful preaching coming forth from their pulpits, usually emphasizing discipleship and the lordship of Christ. Many of these churches have a prophetic ecosystem that produces many people who can prophesy with the revelatory gifts in activation.[197] They often have a mid-sized church (roughly 300-500 people in the U.S.A) because the services are longer than seeker-sensitive churches. They are larger than pastoral and teaching churches because of the excitement of vision and abundance of revelation, but they usually don't become megachurches because of the length of the Sunday services and inconsistency of perpetuating the same vision with simplicity.

Prophets can get bored and will go from one vision or revelation to the next. Prophetic churches regularly need the ministry of the apostle to balance their inspiration with a principled approach to ministry and organization and help the prophet be consistent in perpetuating and casting the same vision to the church. They need the ministry of the evangelist to make the church services become more seeker-sensitive regarding the length of the services and the simple Gospel message needed to win the lost.

Often the prophet's preaching is based on a "rhema" word of the Lord that can lead to sermons on different subjects every week. Thus, the people have a hard time grasping and growing in any one truth of Scripture. Prophets need

---

197   1 Cor. 12:4-11

the ministry of the teacher to understand the need for systematic teaching on Sundays so the church can grow. They need the ministry of the pastor to bring a relational balance so the church can function socially as a community of believers instead of just being a community of people living on spiritual insights and the illumination of the word and prayer.

Evangelists usually gear their whole ministry approach, including Sunday morning services, for the lost. Because they have a heart for people who need the Gospel, they tend to be more seeker-sensitive. They are strong on preaching, exhortation, and soul winning, with a vision to fulfill the Great Commission. The APEST lead pastor has a "gathering anointing" that can attract and inspire huge crowds. Thus, often they have the largest churches in the nations.

Many churches led by an APEST evangelist have "back doors as wide as the front door" because they lack shepherding and small group discipleship. They regularly need the ministry of the teacher to enrich their sermons because their word ministry is often a mile long and an inch deep. They also regularly need the input of a pastor, so the church has a healthy balance between outreach and in-reach.

Evangelist-led churches also need a regular dose of the prophet's ministry to bring the lordship of Christ and commitment to the congregation. While simple salvation messages and motivational messages are great to attract new people to Jesus and the Church, it needs to be balanced with the deeper messages of discipleship. They also need the input of the apostle so the gathering anointing can be harnessed for church planting, cell groups, and organizational strength.

Pastoral churches tend to have an emphasis on in-reach more than outreach. They are very strong on family-related and social events that drive the church, such as church picnics, parties, and other social gatherings meant to deepen relationships and impart a strong covenant community bond. Because they're relationally focused, they have a strong visitation and compassion team replete with hospital visits and other on-site visitation ministries. They may also have a strong counseling ministry with an emphasis on inner healing and emotional health. Their strong teaching emphasis to root and ground the saints in the essentials of the faith.

Often pastoral churches have an informal, community-oriented culture and approach to ministry that sometimes lacks strong vision and administration. They need the ministry of the apostle/teacher to incorporate a culture of excellence regarding protocol and administration. To balance out their informality, they need the ministry of the teacher to impart a love for the word and a formal approach to studying the Scriptures.

APEST pastors, in their compassion for others and desire to help, tend to take on more than they should. They need the ministry and input of the apostle to incorporate a true corporate Kingdom vision. This way, the pastor doesn't just attempt to nurture all the saints without a strategy for training capable saints according to the Pauline strategy for discipleship.[198]

APEST pastors generally focus more on the love and unconditional acceptance of God for all people and often lack strong messages related to the Lordship of Christ. They need the ministry of the prophet to inspire and put fire into the congregation to surrender their lives to the lordship of Christ. They also need the regular ministry of the evangelist to impart to the church a burden to show God's love to those outside the Church as opposed to just those inside the Church.

Churches led by an APEST teacher usually have a strong emphasis on knowing the truth and doctrine. Because of this focus on doctrine, they tend to have strong, high-quality in-reach ministries. They tend to be a very detail-oriented church with great administration and a spirit of excellence in the Sunday services and the way they do ministry.

Teaching churches are usually "a mile deep and an inch wide" with an overemphasis on quality. Because teaching churches don't typically cast a wide net, they need the ministry of the prophet to enlarge the vision of the house. They need the ministry of the apostle to motivate the house to send out ministers to their destiny, instead of just building a strong, stable congregation with no exterior goals. They also need the evangelist to give the church a burden for the lost and outreach. The evangelist can also make the teacher's ministry and teaching approach more amenable to reaching the lost and ministering to babes in Christ.

While doctrine is important for any body of believers, it doesn't always catch the attention of seekers right away. Therefore, the teacher needs the ministry of the prophet/evangelist to put fire in the house to move the Body.

My hope is that everyone who reads this chapter will desire to identify their primary ministry gift and be fully released into their APEST calling. I

---

198   2 Tim. 2:2

also hope many lead pastors, elders, and apostolic leaders will be motivated to utilize the framework of these APEST principles to build healthier and more mature congregations. Finally, I hope that everyone will desire to fully mature in Christ-like character, which is the foundation of the rest of their life instead of merely building upon their anointing and giftings.

May all of us work together for the unity of the faith and use our APEST calling to mature the saints until we come into the fullness of the stature of Jesus Christ. Amen.

CHAPTER 16

THE PROCESS OF PURGING AND REPENTANCE BEFORE PROPHETIC FULFILLMENT

Oftentimes, when we read the Bible or get a word from the Lord, we think that things are going to just happen for us because God said it. But we don't realize the kind of opposition that God uses to test our resolve regarding His plan. We see throughout the Bible that God often visits and judges His people before there is either revival or national judgment. In Genesis, the Triune Godhead visited Abraham as a theophany to prophesy about the children of Abraham and also examine the city of Sodom before enacting judgment.[199] Similarly, Jesus visited the seven churches to conduct an inventory and warn them before He removed their candlestick, a form of His judgment.[200]

Even though the Bible predicted the coming of His everlasting Kingdom thousands of years ago, the people of God had to patiently wait and continue to believe His prophetic words about their glorious future.[201] The Bible promises us that "every knee [will eventually] bow...and every tongue sh[all] confess that Jesus Christ is Lord," and that "[t]he earth will be filled with the knowledge of the glory of the Lord as the waters cover the sea."[202]

---

199   Gen 18-19
200   Rev. 2-3
201   Rom. 8:18-19
202   Phil. 2:5-11; Hab. 2:14

Jesus's triumphal entry into Jerusalem was a prophetic type of how glorious it would have been in Israel had they received Jesus as their Messiah, and it also foreshadowed the glory of all the world submitting to the Lordship of Christ.

The triumphal entry of Jesus into Jerusalem as shown in Matthew 21:1-20 depicts what we call the events of Psalm Sunday:

> *Now when they drew near Jerusalem, and came to Bethphage, at the Mount of Olives, then Jesus sent two disciples, saying to them, "Go into the village opposite you, and immediately you will find a donkey tied, and a colt with her. Loose them and bring them to Me. And if anyone says anything to you, you shall say, 'The Lord has need of them,' and immediately he will send them." All this was done that it might be fulfilled which was spoken by the prophet, saying, "Tell the daughter of Zion, 'Behold, your King is coming to you, lowly, and sitting on a donkey, a colt, the foal of a donkey.'" So the disciples went and did as Jesus commanded them. They brought the donkey and the colt, laid their cloaks, and set Him on them. And a very great multitude spread their clothes on the road; others cut down branches from the trees and spread them on the road. Then the multitudes who went before and those who followed cried out, "Hosanna to the Son of David! Blessed is he who comes in the name of the Lord! Hosanna in the highest!" And when He had come into Jerusalem, all the city was moved, saying, "Who is this?" So the multitudes said, "This is Jesus, from the prophet from Nazareth of Galilee." Then Jesus went into the temple of God and drove out all who bought and sold in the temple, and overturned the tables of the money changers and the seats of those who sold doves. And He said to them, "It is written, 'My house shall be called a house of prayer,' but you make it a 'den of thieves.'" Then the blind and the lame came to Him in the temple, and He healed them. But when the chief priests and the scribes saw the wonderful things that He did, and the children crying out in the temple and saying, "Hosanna to the Son of David!" they were indignant and said to Him, "Do you hear what these are saying?" And Jesus said to them, "Yes. Have you never read,*

*'Out of the mouth of babes and nursing infants You have per-
fected praise?" Then He left them and he went out of the city to
Bethany, and He lodged there.*[203]

Among other things, this narrative shows us that Jesus doesn't just accept
worship from people. He deals with us so we accept Him on His terms; otherwise worship doesn't mean much to Him. He confronted several things that
after they received Him into their city that He still confronts today because
He "is the same yesterday, today, and forever."[204]

When Jesus Comes, He First Purifies His House
When Jesus visits us, He initially gives a glimpse about the future glory
we will share with Him in eternity. This is similar to Palm Sunday. First was
the praise and celebration of His coming, as we see when all Jerusalem worshipped Him with excitement. But then, He came as a refiner's fire to cleanse
the temple because He wants us to worship Him on His terms. The prophetic
word regarding Jesus in Malachi 3:2-5 illustrates this principle:

*"But who can endure the day of His coming? And who can
stand when He appears? For He is like a refiner's fire and like
launderers' soap. He will sit as a refiner and a purifier of silver;
He will purify the sons of Levi, and purge them as gold and
silver, that they may offer to the LORD an offering in righteousness. "Then the offering of Judah and Jerusalem will be
pleasant to the LORD, as in the days of old, as in former years.
And I will come near you for judgment; I will be a swift witness
against sorcerers, against adulterers, against perjurers, against
those who exploit wage earners and widows and orphans, and
against those who turn away an alien..."*[205]

When Christ overturned the tables of the money changers and throw-
ing out the hypocritical religious leaders, He was purifying the Lord's house.

---

203   Matt. 21:1-20
204   Heb. 13:8
205   Mal. 3:2-5

Furthermore, when Jesus overturned the tables of the money changers, it can also be applied in principle to His present-day judgment upon the commercialization of the Gospel. These kinds of judgments are essential before God can visit His House with great power and revival.

Some people get excited when God gives them a prophetic word, but most don't realize that this word is an invitation from God to take them to the next level. This means there must be some things in your past that should be let go, and things in the present that He will confront and deal with. The level of testing we undergo is proportional to the word of the Lord over our life and assignment. For example, regarding the life and trials of Joseph we read, "He had sent a man ahead of them—Joseph—who was sold as a slave. His feet were hurt with fetters, he was laid in irons. Until the time that his word came to pass, the word of the LORD tested him."[206] Practically speaking, if you receive a prophetic word about becoming prosperous, it is an invitation from God to sacrifice, work diligently, get out of debt, give tithes and offerings to God, and study hard to improve your knowledge of wealth management. God doesn't supernaturally rain money upon you from heaven. In the meantime, while you are praying and preparing for wealth, you are likely to be severely tested in your faith regarding your finances.

Not long after the original Triumphal entry into Jerusalem, Jesus spoke about deconstructing the priestly temple system.[207] This was a prediction regarding the future invasion of Roman armies, resulting in the desecration of the temple and destruction of Jerusalem, which took place in 70 A.D. God was doing away with one covenantal system before bringing in a better, more effective covenant built upon better promises.[208] Since then, we have witnessed seasons of God judging His people throughout church history, deconstructing whole ecclesial systems before there was great renewal and awakening. For instance, God purged the church through persecution after its birth on the day of Pentecost before refreshment, renewal, and upswings came to the Kingdom advancement.[209] The post-apostolic church also experienced great hardship and persecution periodically before Constantine was converted in 312 A.D., putting the Church into a place of favor and prominence. Fast for-

206   Ps. 105:17-19

207   Luke 21:5-21

208   Heb. 8:6-13

209   Acts 2:37-40, 3:19, 8:1-3, 9:31

ward twelve hundred years after Constantine, and we see the Roman Catholic Church experience great systemic deconstruction because Jesus was judging the monetization of the gospel through selling indulgences, culminating in the Protestant Reformation. The Reformation became the precondition before many centuries of various renewal movements and gospel expansion was manifest, giving birth to the modern missions movement, evangelical revivals, and the Great Awakenings in the 18th century. Eventually, we come to the twentieth century, yielding Pentecostal movements throughout the world producing various revivals and the unprecedented global expansion of the gospel.

Consequently, these cycles of purging, repentance, and renewal have continued every generation since the biblical narratives of Israel starting with the book of Judges, through the Day of Pentecost to the present-day Church. Truly, Jesus does not merely accept our worship; He purges us so our worship is acceptable to Him based on His own terms and conditions.

God inspects us for fruit.

After His Triumphal entry into Jerusalem, Jesus came back and inspected the fruit on a fig tree. We read, "Now in the morning, as He returned to the city, He was hungry. And seeing a fig tree by the road, he came to it and found nothing on it but leaves, and said to it, 'Let no fruit grow on you ever again!' Immediately the fig tree withered away."[210] This was a metaphor for Him inspecting His people.[211]

This passage illustrates the fact that Jesus expects fruit from His people: the fruit of true spiritual worship, the fruit of the Spirit, the fruit of winning people to Christ, and the fruit of nurturing our families and multiplying disciples and churches. This kind of fruit does not come instantly just because you receive a prophetic word. The word of God teaches us that there is a mean, tough process, and we have to endure times of testing before we are prepared for the prophetic words to come to pass.

When He didn't find fruit, He eventually cursed the fig tree, like He did the nation of Israel when they rejected Him.[212] In Matthew 21:43-44, He

---

210 Matt. 21:18-19
211 Is. 6:9-13
212 Matt. 21:43-44

said, "Therefore I say to you, the kingdom of God will be taken from you and given to a nation bearing the fruits of it. And whoever falls on this stone will be broken; but on whomever it falls, it will grind him to powder." This is not a prophetic game! We can't just say yes to God and think that satisfies Him! He is not fooled with our tears and fake prayers of commitment; He demands progress and fruit by internally transforming believers through His love so they can continue conforming to His image.[213]

Others will subtly or overtly challenge our authority.

Not only does God inspect our fruit, but others will also challenge our calling and assignment. Even Jesus's authority was questioned when He walked out His purpose.[214] To a lesser degree, the place God has called us to walk in will also be challenged. For example, every prophetic word I have ever received from the Lord has been challenged by at least one of the following:

1. My own thoughts. I sometimes question whether I have the right to carry out the Word. The greatest strongholds opposing God's will are in our own thoughts and imaginations.[215] If I have low self-esteem or expect failure, my biggest challenge is my own self-doubt and or unbelief in God's Word.

2. Satanic interference. There will be spiritual warfare opposing you at every step toward progress, especially when you start to change in the beginning. This is a great sign and means that you are on the right path![216]

3. Other people not coming through on their promises. Circumstances seem to go against every prophetic word. For example, you receive a word about having a healing ministry but you get sick the next day, or a word about prosperity and then you lose your job. These are all tests to see if our authority is in our circumstances or by faith in the God who gave us the word of prophecy. Notice how

213   2 Cor. 3:18
214   Luke 20:1-2
215   2 Cor. 10:3-5
216   Eph. 6:10-13; James 4:7

Jesus did not tell people how He received His authority.[217] He never stooped to defending Himself or got upset because others didn't receive Him. His faith was in His Father.

Finally, we all have to be proven before we can be trusted in ministry.[218] We have to earn trust by a period of faithfulness. After a long season of consistency, we must prove our calling to ourselves, our family, friends, and those in authority over us before our primary assignment can begin.

One of the things that will enable us to keep going in spite of all our challenges is the biblical hope in the fact that eventually Light will overcome the darkness as the kingdoms of this world become the kingdom of our Lord and His Christ.[219] The Light of Christ will conquer all darkness.

217   Luke 20:8
218   1 Tim. 3:1-10
219   John 1:5; Rev. 11:15

CHAPTER 17

WHY THE PROPHETIC LIGHT WILL EVENTUALLY OVERCOME THE DARKNESS

God promises that our light shines the greatest in the midst of gross darkness. Isaiah 60:1-2 says:

> Arise, shine; for your light has come! And the glory of the Lord
> is risen upon you. For behold, the darkness shall cover the earth,
> and deep darkness the people; but the Lord will arise upon you,
> and His glory will be seen upon you. The Gentiles shall come to
> your light, and kings to the brightness of your rising.

This amazing passage illustrates the principle that God sometimes displays His Glory in the most challenging times in a culture and society. The Apostle Paul put it another way when he said, "...where sin abounded, grace abounded much more."[220] Truly, those who understand God's ways know that every challenge is an opportunity to elevate our capacity.

In this context, John 1:1-7 gives us several reasons why the Light will eventually overcome all Darkness. In this passage, we understand light to be a metaphor for God's truth and darkness a metaphor for the distortion of truth through the evil one and his fallen systems of earthly governance. Understanding this principle is important in the meta-narrative of this book, because in the midst of believing both the prophetic God-breathed word of the Scriptures, as well as personal prophetic words we can use to wage war, we need to have hope in the ultimate victory of the Light over darkness.[221]

---

220   Rom. 5:20b
221   2 Pet. 1:29-21; 1 Tim. 1:18.

John 1:1 says, "In the beginning was the Word, and the Word was with God, and the Word was God." The word "beginning" (*arche* in Greek) was a classical Greek term which referred to philosophers trying to define the "stuff" out of which emanated the material universe. In Greek, the "Word" or *logos* referred to the wisdom, logic, and ideas underpinning the cosmos. John 1:1-3 teaches us here that Jesus—the *logos* or wisdom of God—is the origin of all living and nonliving things; the knowledge and language of God—who created time and space by His spoken word—runs through all reality like a thread through a tapestry.[222] Even our human DNA, scientists discovered, is composed of what they call "the language of God," which determines our cellular structure, as well as who and what we become.[223]

From eternity, Jesus had a purpose for each of us even before we had a human body! This is what Paul referred to when he wrote that Jesus "... saved us and called us with a holy calling, not according to our works, but according to His own purpose and grace which was given to us...before time began..."[224] Since Jesus created all things and made us in His image, it is possible that each individual is the result of a prophetic word God spoke over them from eternity through the Messiah Jesus.[225] Consequently, since you exist; you have a purpose. You were not merely born—you were sent! Light will eventually overcome all darkness because the *logos* is the foundation for all creation reality.

Furthermore, the Light will overcome the darkness because, as natural knowledge and learning increase, logic and reason will eventuate in the dissipation of atheistic evolution and the worldwide scientific embrace of the Creator.[226] Truly, creation reflects the glory of God whose complexities in design point to the Creator.[227] John tells us that all life arises out of Christ: "He was in the beginning with God. All things were made through Him, and

---

222   Gen. 1:1; Heb. 11:3; Ps. 19:1-6

223   Francis Collins, *The Language of God*, New York: Free Press, 2007.

224   2 Tim. 1:9

225   John 1:3; Gen. 1:27

226   "Center for Science and Culture," Discovery Institute, accessed March 29, 2021, https://www.discovery.org/id/about/. On the Discovery Institute website, you can find out more on how the advances of science prove the existence of a divine Creator through the Intelligent Design theory.

227   Ps. 19:1-6; Rom. 1:19-23.

without Him nothing was made that was made."[228] As the fields of geology, anthropology, cosmology, biology, zoology, and so on get more acute and sophisticated, the complexities and beauty of the creation design will overthrow materialistic presuppositions, resulting in a wave of scientists converting to a belief in intelligent design. Consequently, the light will overcome the darkness because new scientific findings will be broadcast on social media, awakening a new generation of God-seekers and sparking a global revival of young people coming to Jesus.

"In Him was life, and the life was the light of all men."[229] The Greek word for life is "zoë," which, in Scripture, refers not just to biological life, but also to the spiritual life that originates in Jesus. "Spiritual" here signifies not just conscious existence, but a connection to God, out of which emanates power, purpose, and meaning. All this ultimately points to Jesus, as it exists only in Him. Consequently, light will overcome the darkness because all who earnestly seek for deeper meaning and significance will find the Son.[230] Jesus is the light of all men—not just saved men.[231] This points again to creation grace, or common grace, which leads to Christ. Creation grace is the divine gift that grants civilization the illumination needed for the laws of logic, public administration, economics, politics, the sciences, music, art, and education. This particular grace extends to all; since Jesus created all humans, His APEST DNA is present even in those who don't know Him personally. The light will overcome the darkness because the laws of logic, natural law, and creation grace ultimately lead to Jesus since the created order doesn't make sense without a wise Creator/Designer.

Part of the way Jesus enables civilization to function properly is by utilizing APEST in all members of society so all parts point to Him. (For a further description of how each gift functions in society, see chapter 15.) When Jesus ascended on high, He sanctified and anointed these ministry gifts and sent them back to the church for the purpose of perfecting the saints for the work of the ministry.[232] This means a certain percentage of the population are pioneers and entrepreneurs (apostles). A certain percentage look to the future

---

228   John 1:3
229   John 1:4
230   Jer. 29:11-13
231   John 1:4
232   Eph. 4:7-12

and understand the implications of political, economic, technological and scientific trends (prophets). A certain percentage are good at spreading messages easily (evangelists). A certain percentage explain complex concepts in understandable ways (teachers). And a certain percentage of the population care for and tend people in the greater society (shepherds).

Light will overcome the darkness because the prophetic voice of the church is grounded in the Light of Christ. "The light shines in the darkness, and the darkness did not comprehend it."[233] We know that in its essence, light is more powerful and substantive than darkness. If you light a match in darkness, the light of the flame easily pervades and pierces through it. It easily conquers the darkness surrounding it.

The word John used for "comprehend" is "katalambanō," which means, "to overcome," "to win," "to attain," or "to understand." John used this word to illustrate how the Light will ultimately overcome the darkness. The darkness cannot attain or defeat the light, as it is the weaker opponent. However, it's also not just weaker in power, but in intelligence. By saying the darkness can't comprehend or understand the light, John implies that since darkness cannot fully grasp or attain to the light, the Light is more sophisticated, cunning, and greater than darkness. Thankfully, through the process of time and the progress of human history, the light of the Kingdom of God will continue to advance and increase until darkness is fully consumed.[234] The Bible speaks about a time in the future when the effects of the gospel will be so great, it will dramatically increase longevity and the quality of life for everyone.[235] Historically, the advent of Christianity has greatly advanced the quality of life in many nations of the world, especially the West. The advent of modern science, universities, the abolition of slavery, modern concepts of religious freedom, music composition, the rule of law, social justice, human government, and much more emanated out of Christ-followers who impacted their world, especially in the Western Hemisphere.[236] Even today, we have seen a

---

233   John 1:5

234   Is. 9:6-7

235   Is. 65:17-25

236   Rodney Stark, *For the Glory of God: How Monotheism Led to Reformations, Witch-Hunts, and the End of Slavery*, Princeton: Princeton University Press, 2004; Rodney Stark, *The Victory of Reason: How Christianity Led to Freedom, Capitalism, and Western Success*, New York: Random House, 2006.

lot of progress in the attempts to beat global poverty; indeed, human progress in areas like medicine and electricity has never been faster.[237]

However, someone needs to strike a match to spread the light around, and we see these people in prophets. John brings up the example of John the Baptist: "There was a man sent from God, whose name was John. This man came for a witness, to bear witness of the Light, that all through him might believe. He was not that Light, but was sent to bear witness of that Light."[238] John the Baptist represented the culmination of the Old Testament prophets and, as such, was the bridge to the Lord Jesus. John also represented all those who have had an experiential encounter with God for the purpose of being a witness of Him.[239]

John also represented the power and truth of the inspired words of these prophets as recorded in sacred Scripture. He had a high view of Scripture; he even claimed to be the one Isaiah prophesied about as the voice crying out in the wilderness preparing the way of the Lord.[240] The recorded Word of God, recognized by the historic Christian church as the sixty-six books included in the canon of Scripture, is amazingly accurate, profound, and authoritative. Peter calls Scripture the surer word of prophecy.[241]

The greatest proof of the Bible is the impossibility of the contrary—which means it has the only world and life view that makes rational sense of human existence and the created order. Even the functional and intellectual atheist and agnostic has to borrow from the biblical worldview of Christian theism to live their life, debate their views, and justify their understanding of goodness, grammar, the laws of logic, categories, the existence of evil, morality, and concepts of right and wrong. For instance, a materialist atheist mourning the loss of a loved one at a funeral borrows from the Christian worldview since, in their worldview, humans have no soul or spirit and are therefore no different from insects they exterminate or the cows they eat as hamburgers.

237   Max Roser and Esteban Ortiz-Ospina, "Global Extreme Poverty," *Our World in Data*, last modified 2019, https://ourworldindata.org/extreme-poverty; Joseph D'Urso, "Human Progress is Faster Than You Think," October 30, 2015, https://www.weforum.org/agenda/2015/10/human-progress-is-faster-than-you-think/.

238   John 1:6-8

239   Matt. 11:13; Acts 1:8

240   Is. 40:3-5

241   2 Pet. 1:19-21

Hence, what rational reason does an atheist have for mourning the loss of a fellow human in a materialistic world?

If there is no God, why should the atheist be concerned about doing the right thing as opposed to the wrong thing? In their worldview, the atheist gets to choose what's right and wrong, not God, the Author of righteousness. Consequently, according to Scripture, every person living a life of rebellion against God is a spiritual fugitive and will be held accountable on the Day of Judgment for living an autonomous life inconsistent with revealed truth and reality. I believe that the light will eventually overcome the darkness because the prophetic voice of the church grounded in the power and fidelity of the Scriptures will overcome all opposition to King Jesus.

John's mission in life was that everyone who heard His preaching would believe in the Messiah "through him."[242] However, since he represented all of the Old Testament prophets and Scriptures, his mission also pointed to the metanarrative of Scripture regarding the ultimate consummation of human history, when all things in heaven and earth will be aligned under Christ.[243] At that time, every knee will bow and every tongue confess that Jesus Christ is Lord.[244] One day, there will be a groundswell of people believing and pointing to Christ, resulting in the restoration of all things spoken by the prophets.[245] This will be the Light's final blow against darkness.

Finally, the light will overcome darkness in our present experience to the extent that we reflect Jesus. In His essence, He is more powerful than darkness and will ultimately overcome darkness on the Day all creation is consummated in Him. May God have the centered prophetic light of Jesus shine through the church more and more until the second bodily return of Messiah manifests. Amen.

242   John 1:7
243   Eph. 1:10.
244   Phil. 2:5-12
245   Acts 3:21

ADDENDUM

In this section, there are a few chapters that deal directly and indirectly with the prophetic, but the content is relevant for all charismatic churches—especially those who flow in the prophetic. It seems to me that charismatic believers seem to be more susceptible to certain strange practices, perhaps because they are more subjective and less biblically grounded. So I wanted to use these pieces to delve into those practices a little more.

SHOULD WE JUDGE THE PROPHETS?

In the past few weeks, some of us have been criticized on social media for having the nerve to call out the prophets for missing it big time regarding COVID and the Trump re-election. Not only did some of them miss it, but instead of apologizing, some prophetic leaders have tried to get off the hook by saying things like:

"Trump really won, but the election was stolen."

"Trump was inaugurated in heaven."

"There are still four more years left. Anything can happen, so I am not apologizing now."

"Trump will be set in around March or April after massive voter fraud is exposed."

"The prophets said Trump would be elected a second term, but they never said it would be two consecutive terms. He will be president in 2024!"

You get the picture.

These kinds of excuses only make things worse. It would have been much better for these prophetic voices to simply admit they missed it instead of digging in their heels.

Furthermore, some people are saying that it is unfair that the prophets are being picked on and that the other ministry gifts should be scrutinized, as well. One man told me on social media that I was maligning the prophets and should have corrected them in private. My friend Dr. Michael Brown told me that he is getting a lot of hate mail for holding some of the prophets accountable. Jeremiah Johnson reportedly received so much vitriolic pushback because he apologized for falsely prophesying a Trump presidential victory that it crashed his website. So again I ask: is it wrong to bring public correction to the prophets?

As a shepherd and a voice to those on my public platforms, I feel obligated to bring correction to false teachings, prophecies, or anything else that's harmful to the people of God or the general public. First of all, it is always within the bounds of protocol to bring public correction to any person who publicly teaches, prophecies, or preaches something misleading to the people of God. Paul actually instructs us to call out spiritual leaders in public under certain situations when their wrong has been verified by at least three credible witnesses.[246] Hence, if a person says something incorrect in public, they should be willing to be corrected in public. Otherwise, they shouldn't release anything again in a public platform. It's important to receive such correction with grace. There's no need to get bent out of shape. Instead, the correction should be seen as an opportunity to grow. If the person giving correction brings up a good point, thank them. If they disagree with you, start a dialogue with them. If they act nasty, don't engage with them.

Secondly, if you do not know the prophet or have a relationship with them, it would be difficult to speak to each of them in private before bringing a public correction. However, Christ's mandate to speak to somebody in private is only in effect if they sinned against you in your personal relationship with that person.[247] Of course, in a local church setting, the judgment of erroneous prophecies is entirely possible and mandated. I recall a new convert to Christ in the very beginning stages of our church began prophesying over everybody he saw—missing it big time in every instance. When I tried to intervene and correct him, he prophesied judgment over me for trying to stop him! I had no choice but to call a meeting with him and the elders and we had to put him out of the church until he repented and submitted to our spiritual oversight.

---

246   1 Tim. 5:19
247   Matt. 18:15-18

Through the years, I have on occasion corrected people who prophesied to our church out of their emotions instead of from the Holy Spirit. One leader once told me that the Holy Spirit told him that I had something against him. I had no idea why he would think that, so I replied, "That is your own insecurities, not the Spirit of God, since I have no issue with you."

All of these erroneous prophetic utterances required a personal intervention from me as the overseer of the congregation. However, those that uttered false prophecies to the nation is not something under my spiritual oversight. Hence, I am not obligated to personally deal with them unless I have a personal relationship with them or they sinned against me.

That being said, the false re-election prophecies did not involve a personal sin against me, but a wrong committed against the tens of thousands of Christians who believed them and had false hope because of them. Whether some prophets misled them intentionally or not, I cannot say or judge, although I think most were sincere but were blinded by their hope for a Trump election.

Paul instructed church leaders to mark those who cause divisions in the church so others will learn from it.[248] He also called out leaders in public when he deemed their words or actions harmful to the church.[249] He called out some who forsook him and left their assignment.[250] Even though I do not believe the intent of many of these prophets was to sow discord, the ensuing confusion in the charismatic church had to be addressed in a public platform. Also, leaders have no way of tracking down and personally connecting with the multiple thousands of confused Christians disillusioned by this prophetic faux paus.

For those who think I am unfairly singling on the prophetic gift can read my book *An Anthology of Essays on Apostolic Leadership*, where I speak about abuse in the apostolic movement. While there is excess and error among all APEST gifts, God commands the prophetic to be judged according to the Scriptures, perhaps more than any other ministry gift.[251] Everybody who teaches, preaches, or prophesies is to be judged more strictly than those who

---

248 Rom. 16:17
249 1 Tim. 1:20; 2 Tim. 4:14
250 2 Tim. 4:9-11
251 Deut. 13:1-5; Jer. 23; 1. Cor. 14:29; 1 John 4:1

do not endeavor to be an oracle for the truth.[252] Thus, those who bring forth the word of God must be very careful to accurately represent the mind and will of God based upon the Scriptures and their exposition of it.[253]

Furthermore, Jesus praised the Ephesian church for "testing those who say they are apostles and are not."[254] Hence, Jesus desires that local churches test their ministry gifts before they validate and recommend their ministry to the Body of Christ.

Finally, the Bible scrutinizes each of the five-fold ministries, not just the prophetic, although the very nature of the prophetic demands strict judgment since the one prophesying claims the Lord speaks through them. The Bible says that any of the APEST ministry gifts can fall into deception. Even sincere, godly Christians—including prophetic leaders—can make mistakes and unintentionally mislead masses of people through their social media platform. Consequently, it behooves the Church to collectively respond online to false teachings and judge prophetic words, bringing greater balance to the Church for the glory of God. When bringing correction, may we treat each other with grace, kindness, and mercy as we await the coming of our Lord and Savior Jesus Christ.

---

252 James 3:1
253 1 Pet. 4:11
254 Rev. 2:2

TEN SIGNS OF CHARISMANIA

As a believer with a Pentecostal background, I have seen many genuine moves of God, as well as many counterfeits works of the flesh. Unfortunately, many believers lack the discernment to tell the difference between what is of God and what originates with man.

My grandmother was the pastor of a classical Pentecostal Hispanic church for over fifty years. Through that experience, I was able to understand some Pentecostal roots and practices. Generally speaking, the ethnic classical Pentecostals I have come across (Italian, Spanish, African American, Russian, to name a few) were known to be very strict when it came to outward holiness, to the point that many of us called them legalistic. For example, there was no dancing, no entertainment, and no movies. Women could not wear pants or make-up or cut their hair, and even the men had a strict dress code of wearing a suit and a tie.

Out of the original Pentecostal movement arose the Charismatic movement of the 1960s and 1970s, in which the historic denominational churches received the baptism of the Holy Spirit with the evidence of speaking in other tongues. Because of the legalism associated with the word "Pentecostal," many evangelicals across denominational lines have since felt more comfortable using the term "charismatic" to describe their Pentecostal experience—including speaking in tongues, believing in divine healing, and deliverance from demonic oppression. When evangelicals such as C. Peter Wagner and John Wimber received the baptism of the Spirit, they distinguished themselves from charismatics and Pentecostals because they did not believe speaking in tongues was always necessary to validate the second blessing. Consequently, they referred to the movement they helped usher in as the "Third Wave"—something that I resonate with personally. However, in the past decade I have witnessed so much excess in some charismatic circles that I have also felt uncomfortable at times using the term "charismatic" to describe my Pentecostal leanings. Consequently, I use the term "Reformed Charismatic" to describe my expression of Christianity because standalone terms such as "Pentecostal" and "charismatic" have a certain kind of baggage associated with them.

A classical charismatic and/or Pentecostal, in the way I define them, is a person who has received Christ as Lord and Savior, who stands upon the word of God as the final authority, and who also believes in the manifestations of the Spirit as found in 1 Corinthians 12:4-8, as well as the gift of speaking in tongues as found in 1 Corinthians 14:2, 4. Charismatics and Pentecostals typically listen to the voice of God in congruence with the Scriptures inside their spirit to give them specific guidance as opposed to some fundamentalist evangelicals who believe God only speaks through the written pages of the Bible.

There are other distinctions I could mention. Through the years, some with the charismatic experience have become so subjective they have embraced "wildfire" and given charismatics a bad reputation. This is one of the reasons notable fundamentalist cessationist John MacArthur and others have hosted conferences dealing with "strange fire" related to the charismatic movement. However, I am skeptical of a critique coming from a person historically biased against Pentecostals. I would rather hear a critique from a practicing charismatic or Pentecostal.

Thankfully, the vast majority of charismatics I walk with do not believe or practice any of the following. However, some strange practices have indeed infiltrated the charismatic Church. The following ten erroneous beliefs are signs you are involved in charismania.

1. **You put prophecies and extra-biblical experiences on the same level as the written word of God.**

Isaiah 8:20 says if we speak not according to the Scripture then we have no light. 2 Timothy 3:16 teaches that all Scripture is inspired by God and "profitable for doctrine, for reproof, for correction, for instruction in righteousness." The Scriptures are our rule for life and the highest standard for judging truth.

Unfortunately, some in the charismatic camp seem to be led more by personal prophecies and supernatural visions and dreams than by the Scriptures. I have known some people who would record personal prophecies by well-known "prophets" and—without praying about it, comparing it to Scripture, or getting discerning counsel from more seasoned leaders in the Kingdom—would just obey the prophecy as if it were as inspired as the Bible!

There are some others who seem to get daily visions and dreams from God that guide them. While I do believe God can speak through visions and dreams, we have to be careful because Satan also comes as an angel of light and can deceive naïve believers.[255] Just because they have a supernatural encounter doesn't mean it's from the Lord. Paul said, "even if...an angel from heaven[] preach[es] any other gospel...let him be accursed."[256] The surer word of prophecy comes from the inspired writings of the canonical books of both the Old and New Testaments, which should be our guiding light for life and by which all prophetic utterances should be judged.[257]

If a prophetic word or supernatural vision doesn't go against the Scriptures, we still need to pray and get a witness from the Lord in our spirit. The Scriptures cannot always give us specific guidance, but it can always provide general principles and precepts. We also need to get counsel from mature leaders as to whether this prophetic word or vision really is specific guidance from Him.

Lest my non-charismatic friends gloat over this point, let me say that a totally objective human being does not and cannot exist. As I said in a previous chapter -all humans are subjective, even the non-charismatics who believe God only speaks to us through the Bible. The only truly objective being in the universe is God because He is the only one who is never influenced by time, space, or environment! Even fundamentalist cessationists are subjective because they believe they are saved because they have "a witness [in] their spirit" that they are children of God.[258]

Since we can't avoid subjectivity, how do we determine biblical truth? The only way to know the truth is to trust that the Holy Spirit will guide us and our leaders into all truth when we study the Scriptures. We also have a responsibility to read how the believing church has historically interpreted the word down through the centuries. When there is a consensus from the

255   2 Cor. 11:14
256   Gal. 1:8.
257   2 Pet. 1:19-21
258   Rom. 8:16

historic orthodox evangelical Church regarding the interpretation of a passage or truth of the Bible, then we can have general assurance that the Holy Spirit has illuminated this truth to His people.[259]

2. You are blindly led by charismatic leaders.

Though this can be the case for the non-charismatic world as much as the charismatic world, as a Third wave charismatic, I am going to pick on my own camp. I have seen far too many believers get caught up in following the teachings of charismatic leaders, even if their leaders are not living moral lives. There have also been leaders who endorse political candidates who push anti-biblical laws and many charismatics not only follow them, but vote like them.

There have also been charismatics getting divorced and remarrying for unbiblical reasons or living opulent lifestyles with no accountability. But, because they have "charisma," move in the gifts of the Spirit, and have a great preaching anointing, people follow them without question. Many churches have devolved into nothing more than personality cults and are led by charismatic leaders who could preach heresy with much of their church still shouting amen and hallelujah!

On the Day of Judgment, God will hold each of us accountable for our lives, our families, and our callings. We will not be able to give an excuse for being led astray by a leader if we have not taken the time to study the Scriptures and seek God for ourselves.

3. You come to church looking for experiences more than Jesus.

Many in charismatic churches come to church to "feel" God's presence because it makes them feel good. That is all good and fine for new believers, but we must get to where we want to know the person of God and not just feel the presence of God. For example, I want to know my wife's heart, not just smell her perfume or feel her physical embrace. Only when we know God can we make Him known.[260]

---

259   St. Vincent of Lerins, *The Commonitory of St. Vincent of Lerins*, CreateSpace, 2012.
260   John 17:3

4. You think weird physical gyrations or manifestations are necessary to experience to be "in the Spirit."

There have been some so-called revivals or renewal movements in Pentecostal and charismatic churches, even in classical Pentecostal churches, in which people think the Holy Spirit is moving upon a person because they start jerking, going into weird gyrations, barking like a dog, clucking like a chicken, dancing in the Spirit, running, spinning, etc. When I first preached in a classical Pentecostal church, I thought someone was having an epileptic attack. But then someone told me it was the Holy Ghost upon them!

While I am sure the Holy Spirit does at times move upon us in such a way that we can have a strong physical, emotional, and psychological reaction to the raw power and presence of God (which has happened to me on several occasions), I am convinced that many people try to manufacture a move of God upon themselves that is nothing more than hype and a work of the flesh.

God does not have to operate in such a manner to speak to us or move upon us. Some of my most powerful experiences in Christ have been hearing His gentle, "still small voice" during times of intimate worship, or just fellowshipping with Him as I went about my daily routine.[261]

In my opinion, sometimes unstable people, in their zeal for God, give in to their emotions and manifest weirdness in the name of the Lord, which is nothing but a work of the flesh, and in some cases can be demonic. Furthermore, I have seen whole churches celebrate these weird manifestations as moves of God, resulting in attracting emotionally unstable charismatics from other churches with very few unbelievers getting converted.

5. You focus on soaking in the Spirit rather than being empowered by the Spirit to be a witness.

According to Acts 1:8, the primary purpose of Spirit baptism is to be empowered to be a witness of the resurrection of Christ. Thus, the power of the Spirit has a missional focus, not a self-centered focus. Many charismatics think the Spirit has come upon them to make them feel good and all they want to do is come to church to "soak in the presence of God." But my Bible

---

261   1 Kings 19:13.

teaches me that every single time a human being encountered the presence of God, it resulted in God sending out that person to do work for His Kingdom. God sent Moses to lead His people out of Egypt after speaking to him from a burning bush.[262] We see God sending Isaiah out after the prophet encountered Him in His courts.[263] After having a vision of the Lord's glory, Ezekiel was sent to preach to Israel in her rebellion.[264] Upon his encounter with Jesus on the road to Damascus, Paul was sent to minister to the Gentiles.[265] Unfortunately, Charismaniacs are focused on soaking themselves in a good feeling, not on being sent by God.

The book of Acts could also be called the book of the Holy Spirit because the Spirit is active in every aspect of the work of the Church. The book's focus is action, not feelings, or even teachings. It's called the Book of Acts for a reason! Even when the Antiochian church was corporately worshipping God, the Holy Spirit sent out two of their best leaders to preach the gospel.[266]

6. You are mystical and are not practical.

The Bible is the most practical book in the world about being a steward of the things of God on earth. It is not a book about heaven, nor is it focused on mystical things. Hence, when we are solely heavenly-minded, we are of earthly good.[267]

Many charismatics are constantly interpreting numbers and analyzing life sequences, dreams, and visions, spiritualizing everything to the point in which they don't accomplish very much on the earth! To this day many are spending hours trying to decode conspiracy theories like QAnon, interpret the significance of the Hebrew calendar (which can be a form of Kabbalah), and wasting countless hours speculating about the last days and the rise of the Antichrist!

In my opinion, every spiritual or mystical experience that does not directly result in either a person knowing God more intimately or being equipped to

---

262   Ex. 3:1-16
263   Is. 6
264   Ezek. 1:28-2:13
265   Acts 9; 22:14-15
266   Acts 13:1-2
267   Col. 3:1-3

serve Him better in this world is a waste of time and not worth their atten- tion. Charismatics would be better served if they focused on understanding the first principles of the faith.[268] It would also be beneficial to limit their time on Facebook and spend the bulk of their time poring over His Book, which alone will give them the discernment they need to live a fruitful, godly life.

7. You claim to speak to the saints in heaven.

I have heard some leaders who have claimed to have conversations with the Old Testament patriarch Abraham and the Apostle Paul and other de- parted saints of old. They justify this by claiming we are surrounded by the "cloud of witnesses," which includes the departed saints.[269] A witness, some say, is someone who speaks; hence, the saints of old can bear witness to us re- garding the will of God. However, this same passage also tells us to look unto Jesus—not to the departed saints.[270] There is no passage in the Bible related to the post-ascension Church that validates this kind of communication. Furthermore, necromancy (conjuring up the dead)—also called "divination," "sorcery," and "spiritism"—is forbidden many times in Scripture.[271] This is dangerous and can lead to the saint worship heresy of the Roman Catholic tradition. 1 Timothy 2:5 says, "…there is one God and one Mediator between God and men, the Man Jesus Christ." I don't need to speak to Paul, Mary, Abraham, or any of the saints of old. Jesus assigned the Holy Spirit to guide us into all truth and to reveal that truth to us.[272] Not even a heaven-abiding Paul the Apostle could do better than the Holy Spirit!

Some may also point out that Moses and Elijah appeared to Jesus to speak of His coming death, thus validating their practice of speaking to the departed saints.[273] However, this narrative in the gospels was a special appearance related to the fact that Moses (representing the law) and Elijah (representing the prophets) both pointed to Jesus as the Messiah, thus validat-

268 Heb. 6:1-3
269 Heb. 12:1-2
270 Heb. 12:2
271 Lev. 19:26; Deut. 18:10; Gal. 5:19-20
272 John 14:26; 16:14
273 Luke 9:29-31

ing His coming to the Jewish people.[274] It has nothing to do with having visions of talking to saints.

8. You claim frequent angelic visitations.

Once, I was asked to conduct a television interview with a person called the "Angel Lady." I turned it down because I did not want my name associated with this nonsense. I also would not have been a good host, but would have seriously challenged her views and unintentionally humiliated her in public. Her ministry reportedly had to do with helping people connect to their "guardian angel." However, I don't need anyone teaching me how to connect to my "guardian angel." The only angel I earnestly seek is the Angel of the Lord, who "encamps around those who fear Him," whom many scholars believe is none other than Jesus Christ.[275]

Although I know I have angels going before me when I do the work of the Kingdom, it is not my responsibility to get to know them or give them orders. The word of God teaches me to "grow in the grace and knowledge of our Lord and Savior Jesus Christ" and never admonishes me to get to know my guardian angel.[276] This kind of foolishness can lead to angelic worship, which the Apostle Paul said would disqualify us.[277] Although Hebrews 1:14 says that angels are sent to serve believers, Psalm 91:11 teaches that God is the one who commands them, not us. Giving angels orders bypasses the protocol of prayer that instructs us to approach the Father in the name of Jesus when we have a need for something.[278] The Bible says nothing regarding believers speaking or commanding angels. God is the Lord of Hosts and He knows best how to dispense His angelic army!

I have met and or heard about many who claim to have frequent angelic visitations and encounters. Of course, we have to admit that angels played a prominent role at times in the early Church. (See the angelic visitation to the Roman centurion Cornelius in Acts 10; Peter's angelic rescue from prison in Acts 12:5-19; and the angel who appeared to Paul to encourage him in

---

274   Luke 24:25-27
275   Ps. 34:7
276   2 Pet. 3:18
277   Col. 2:18
278   John 16:23-24

his seafaring journey in Acts 27:21-25.) The Scriptures also admonish us to entertain strangers, knowing that some of them may be angelic beings.[279] However, those mentioned in the Acts narratives above were going about proclaiming the Gospel and risking their lives for His kingdom. The bottom line is, the claim of angelic visitations are only credible commensurate to the resulting fruit borne for the Kingdom.

9. You lack biblical depth and doctrinal soundness.

Few are the saints in the church that are like the Bereans who searched the Scriptures to see whether what Paul the Apostle preached was true![280] Charismaniacs are driven by subjective feelings and very rarely crack open the Bible for serious study. I have also been with prophetic leaders who merely "share" what the Lord has given them without even attempting to preach out of the Bible! The less knowledge of the word you have, the less discernment you will have to vet whether the thoughts and imaginations coming into your brain are from the Lord or from the devil.[281] Thus, charismaniacs are susceptible to false teachings and false prophets who can deceive them with false signs and wonders and unbiblical teachings.[282]

Jesus told the Sadducees that they were in error because they knew not the Scriptures nor the power of God.[283] In my opinion, Jesus constantly quoted throughout the gospels to give us an example. Scripture has to frame our life and supernatural encounters so we can have proper discernment! No Scripture equals no discernment, and no discernment equals potential deception.[284]

10. You are independent from the Body of Christ because you are "led by the Spirit."

I have known several charismaniacs who are not connected to any one local church but just float around from church to church because, they told

---

279   Heb. 13:2
280   Acts 17:10-11
281   2 Cor. 10:3-5
282   2 Cor. 11:13-15
283   Matt. 22:29
284   Heb. 5:12-14

me, they are "being led by the Spirit." I have even heard of several social media prophets who don't think they need to be a part of a local church! Furthermore, I heard some so-called prophets even think submitting to a pastor in a local church is beneath them, since they believe prophets to be a higher authority on the APEST hierarchical scale than pastors.

Disconnected, non-submissive people like this will never fully maximize their potential in the Lord because, like a seed, you have to be planted in the ground to reach your potential. Psalm 92:13 says that being planted in the house of the Lord precedes flourishing. Even Jesus needs a body to fulfill His present mission.[285] Those not connected and committed to a church are like a person who dismembered their hands and then expects them to function on their own!

My intent is not to throw the baby out with the bathwater here. The vast majority of charismatic/Pentecostal believers I know love the Lord. Without the charismatic/Pentecostal camp, I honestly believe the Church would be dead and on the road to extinction by now. It is these kinds of churches that are expanding global Christianity. That being said, it is time for the Church to embrace the true purpose of Pentecost and discard foolishness that will hinder Kingdom advancement.[286] It is time for us to shake off these beliefs that "ensnare us" and to run unhindered "the race that is set before us."[287]

---

285 Eph. 1:22-23
286 Acts 1:8
287 Heb. 12:1

STRANGE TEACHINGS THAT HAVE CREPT INTO THE CHURCH

In my years of pastoring, I have seen and heard many off-the-wall and aberrant teachings. Some stick out more than others to me. The following are ten unbalanced and strange teachings that have crept into the charismatic church:

1. Double portion services.

These are church services in which the preacher promises that every person they lay hands on, or who gives a certain amount of money, will receive a double portion of the anointing. However, in only one instance in Scripture did a person receive a double portion from another person. In 2 Kings 2, Elisha received a double portion of the spirit that was upon his mentor, Elijah the prophet.[288] But this was not merely an event, but rather the culmination of years of Elisha following and serving Elijah. When Elijah was taken up, Elisha received that which was rightfully his because of his time faithfully serving and learning from his spiritual father. Hence, it was not an event, but a process that culminated in an impartation of the double portion.

Those who teach that you can receive a double portion of the anointing or a blessing by merely showing up to a meeting and getting hands laid upon them negate the fact that Elisha left everything to follow Elijah and that this also involved hard arduous work, humility and discipline over a period of year.

---

288   2 Kings 2:9-15

2. Hundred-Fold Financial Blessing

Some teach that if you give a certain amount of money to their ministry, you will receive a "hundredfold" blessing in return. They get this from the passage in Mark 10:29-30: "So Jesus answered and said, 'Assuredly, I say to you, there is no one who has left house or brothers or sisters or father or mother or wife or children or lands, for My sake and the gospel's who shall not receive a hundredfold now in this time—houses and brothers and sisters and mothers and children and lands, with persecutions—and in the age to come, eternal life.'"

First of all, Jesus is telling this to His followers who left everything for Him. This is not a promise for someone who only puts money into an offering bucket. Second, a "hundredfold blessing," as some interpret it, means that if a person puts one dollar in the offering, he will get a hundred dollars back. Ten dollars will retrieve him one thousand dollars, one thousand dollars will result in a one hundred thousand return and a one hundred-thousand-dollar investment will result in a $10 million return. While God does generously bless us back when we give to Him, I don't believe He was literally promising a hundredfold financial blessing to every person who gives. The context of this passage was that everyone who leaves their home and their family to minister for Christ will have a hundredfold blessing of receiving countless spiritual fathers, mothers, sisters, brothers, and numerous houses where they can stay. I have experienced this firsthand. I have traveled the world for Christ and now have countless people I consider part of my spiritual family in Christ.

Using this passage to get people to invest money in their ministry is misleading and confusing to people who will most likely never really see a hundredfold return on their giving.

3. Grave sucking

In recent years, there has been a craze in which Christians will go to the grave of a great saint, like Charles Finney, and lay on top of his grave to get some of the anointing of this departed hero in the faith. This practice comes from a misinterpretation and consequent misapplication of 2 Kings 13:21, in which a dead man was accidentally thrown into the grave of Elisha and came back to life after the corpse touched the bones of the great prophet.

First of all, there is no mention in Scripture that the man received the anointing of Elisha to minister. Second, there is no mention that the people of God made a ritual out of this practice so other people can be revived and or receive power from the bones of Elisha. This was a one-time miracle that was probably meant to remind and warn Israel as to the veracity and power of the dead prophet's words that were still yet to come to pass.

Charismatics often want a shortcut to the anointing. It is not going to come just because a person lies on a grave, throws a jacket upon you, and or lays hands upon you. It comes by waiting upon the Lord, studying His word, seeking His face, and sitting under the mentorship of leaders called to equip you in the work of the ministry.

4. Open Theism[289]

The controversial view of divine knowledge known as "open theism" is increasingly being taught, debated, and proposed by serious men and women in the church. Proponents of this view claim that the classical theistic view regarding God's omniscience is wrong and that an honest reading of Scripture clearly shows that in certain instances, God limits his insight into the future so that He does not know everything that will happen. I have attended conferences, read papers, and witnessed passionate arguments over this so-called "doctrine" for the past several years. Presently, there are also variants of this teaching that claim to make it different from open theism like "Father/Son theology." However, they all come from the same source as open theism, so if you refute one, then like a domino effect all its variant teachings also fall.

I strongly disagree with this view and, while I respect and honor some of the leaders who have advanced, argued for, and taught open theism, I am greatly concerned that any movement that promotes this teaching will lose its credibility with the rest of the Body of Christ. In my opinion, open theism goes against the historic views of the church with respect to omniscience, which is one of God's main attributes.

This new concept of God is similar to some aspects of pantheism (that God is one with His creation) and process theology (that God is still growing in

---

289   Joseph Mattera, "The Case Against Open Theism," jospehmattera.org, January 8, 2008, https://josephmattera.org/the-case-against-open-theism/.

knowledge and power with His creation, like a form of Darwinian divinity). It is an ultra-extreme form of Arminianism regarding free will; thus, it is a threat to Christian orthodox belief.

The whole system collapses once it fails to answer the theological question demanded by Revelation 13:8, which teaches Jesus was "slain from the foundation of the world." Obviously, this shows that God was not surprised by the fall of Adam and already had the cross in mind before He made Adam and the world. God's supposed surprise by mankind's fall demonstrates that anthropomorphic language is often used as a divine bridge so man can relate to God as a person.[290] Hence, all the other similar passages proponents of open theism use to prove that God does not know the future is a straw house that collapses under the weight of this and many other passages that show infinite Divine foreknowledge.

Proponents of open theism believe that their open view of the future alleviates God of the responsibility for evil in the world. But what they do not take into account is that, even within their own system, God is just as responsible because He created beings that He knew were potentially going to sin, thus making God an accessory before and after the fact. Despite their denials, God is still responsible for evil because He did not use His omnipotent power to stop His beings from sinning even though He knew the potential for it in the future.

In both these points, God's passive permission in extreme Arminianism is basically the same as proactive causality, or hyper-Calvinism, thus rendering the essence of open theism basically no different from the hyper-Calvinistic views they oppose.

5. Full preterism

Full preterism is the doctrine that teaches all biblical prophecies, including the second bodily return of Christ, have already been fulfilled. Without getting into detail regarding this view, I will only say here that this teaching can de-motivate its adherents regarding global evangelization and transformation since, according to this view, everything Jesus promised has already been fulfilled. Also, this view goes against both the Nicene Creed and the Apostles' Creed, which state the orthodox belief that Jesus will return bodily to judge the living and the dead.[291]

---

290 Gen. 3:8-19

291 Joseph Mattera, "The Strengths and Weaknesses of the Main Views of Eschatology

6. Hyper-grace[292]

Proponents of hyper grace teach that the moral law found in the Ten Commandments has no relevance in the New Testament Church era. This leads to the heresy of antinomianism (meaning "without law;" we will review this in more depth later in this chapter), which eradicates all biblical standards and ethics. Consequently, its proponents can theoretically sin without fear, as everything is based on grace without consideration for the moral law of God. Some even teach that since Jesus died for all your past, present, and future sins, you don't even need to confess your sins because that is work and not grace, to which I would point them to 1 John 1:9.

Whenever a church only preaches the love and blessings of God in Christ without ever mentioning the need to repent and or the consequences of sin in the life of the believer, then there is a good chance that it is a hyper-grace church.

7. Hyper-Zionism

Although I believe in the future restoration of all Israel, I don't base my life and ministry upon the political restoration of the nation of Israel.[293] Hyper-Zionist believers have a hyper-dispensational view of biblical prophecy that renders the church as second-class citizens to people of biological Jewish origin, whether they are followers of Jesus the Messiah or not. Everything they preach and do revolves around political Israel. As an example, I remember one time in a city-wide prayer gathering, a national prophetic figure put cold water on a powerful meeting when he said that unless we minister to the Jew first, revival will not come to our churches and our regions. After that statement, the whole meeting died.

I believe in ministering to Jewish people and that our nation should be a strong ally with political Israel. However, I also believe strongly in ministering to the Arab people; hence I do not center my whole ministry upon the

(The Last Days)," josephmattera.org, December 12, 2016. https://josephmattera.org/the-strengths-and-weaknesses-of-the-main-views-of-eschatology-the-last-days/.

292   Joseph Mattera, "Eight Signs of Hyper Grace Churches," josephmattera.org, October 13, 2017. https://josephmattera.org/eight-signs-of-hyper-grace-churches-2/. My article on this subject goes into more depth.

293   Rom. 11:26-27

restoration of the Jew. God has greatly blessed our church and ministry as He has thousands of other churches and leaders throughout church history who never focused their whole life and ministry in Jewish evangelism or the restoration of political Israel. Of course, God never blesses anti-Semitism, and He still has a special place in His heart for Jewish people and the land of Israel that I believe will one day be restored as a joy to the whole earth.

8. Hyper-Deliverance

There are some leaders in the church who believe that the remedy for every ailment, both emotional and physical, is deliverance. By "deliverance," I mean the act of dispelling demons from a person's life. Although there is definitely a need for casting out demons as Jesus commanded, we need to discern when there is a need to pray for healing, when there is only a need for repentance from works of the flesh, and when the primary culprit is demonic in nature.[294]

Some churches have gone so far off a deep end in deliverance that they actually hand out doggie bags to attendees so they can cough out demons during the service. People were taught to come every Sunday to have demons cast out of them instead of teaching them how to walk with God, stay filled with the Holy Spirit, and maintain their deliverance. How will they learn to walk out their faith in the Lord if they rely on a church service to be exorcised? The Bible teaches believers that the devil will flee from them if they resist him.[295] Jesus told his followers that He gave them power over the enemy.[296] Christ followers are also expected to cast down every imagination or thought that sets itself up against the knowledge of God.[297] Paul told the church to put on the whole armor of God during the day of evil.[298] Consequently, if a Christian is not taught to resist demonic attacks, they will always remain a babe in Christ who continually depends upon others to resist the devil for them.

---

294 Mark 16:17
295 James 4:7
296 Luke 10:17-20
297 2 Cor. 10:3-5
298 Eph. 6:10-18

9. Hyper-Prophetic

As already mentioned in this book, many people base their life's direction and ministry upon prophetic words they receive from other leaders. Although I believe and rely strongly on the prophetic, by hearing God's voice through another individual or to my own spirit, I have seen extremes in this movement. I have been to some church services in which there were more than a dozen people giving words, even though Paul tells us in 1 Corinthians 14:29 that only two or at the most three prophets should speak in one service.

I don't care how well known or accurate a prophet is, I will never obey a word unless God confirms it also to my spirit, because all sons of God are led by the Spirit of God.[299] This is not being disrespectful of the prophetic, but it is being respectful of the Holy Spirit's assignment to guide me into all truth. Of course, every prophetic word has to line up with Holy Scripture. Some act as though prophetic words are on the same level as the Bible, which is a huge error.

Finally, before you make any major decision after receiving a prophecy, always attempt to receive godly counsel from your spiritual leaders who may understand better how to interpret prophetic words and practically apply them in your life. Remember, even the most accurate and well-known prophets in the world can make a mistake, which is why Paul teaches the church to judge every word given.[300]

10. Pelagianism

Pelagianism is the view that Adam did not pass his sin down to his descendants. Proponents of this view teach that humans are born with the potential to live a sinless life—since there was no inherent original sin—although God's grace assisted every good work.[301] According to this view, the Augustinian/reformation understanding of original sin is false.

I have been very disappointed to hear and read present-day teachers who are either full-blown followers of Pelagianism or partial Pelagians. However,

---

299   Rom. 8:14

300   1 Cor. 14:29; 1 Thess. 5:20-21

301   2 Cor. 9:8

this idea is not a new one. Pelagian was a British monk who lived between A.D. 360-418. He taught that humans were not born in original sin and were perfectly able to obey the law of God without divine aid. He taught that humans were prone to sin because of their sinful environment and were not at all affected by the original sin of Adam and Eve.

This view runs contrary to human experience. It is obvious that fleshly selfish tendencies are manifest in all humans from childhood onward. But it also clearly goes against sound doctrine. For example, the Bible teaches us that in our flesh is no good thing, that we are by nature objects of His wrath, and that the human heart is wicked above all other things.[302] Also, Romans 5:12 clearly states that after Adam died, all died. Adam, as the federal head of the human race passed death to all his offspring through sin.

Of course, one of the huge challenges with this teaching is that, in theory, a person can live a sinless life. In that case, even though He is everyone's Lord, Jesus doesn't have to be the Savior of all men like Scripture teaches us in 1 Tim 2:3-4. This violates the whole New Testament. Any teaching that focuses on our ability to serve God through human effort, to the exclusion of the cross and the grace of Christ, is teaching another form of salvation by works, which is another clear violation of biblical teaching.

Of course, Pelagianism is hardly the only ancient heresy infiltrating the Church these days. As a student of church history and theology, I am amazed at the present revival of old heretical views that were already investigated and condemned by the historic, orthodox, universal church. By "heretical," I am referring to teachings unaligned with the clear teachings and accepted belief of Christian orthodoxy taught in Scripture as affirmed by the Bible-believing, historic, orthodox church.

Saint Jude urges us to "contend...for the faith that was once for all delivered unto the saints."[303] Hence, there is a body of biblical doctrine, referred to as "the faith," encompassing the basic beliefs Christ followers should adhere to. If pastors would study some of the writings of the early church fathers who dealt with such things, there would be less ignorance of our historical, biblical theological development, and people would be less prone to being led away with error.

---

302   Rom. 7:14-20; Eph. 2:1-2; Jer. 17:9

303   Jude 3

THE OLD HERESIES

1. Antinomianism

This term was first coined by Martin Luther in his 1539 book *Against the Antinomians*, derived from placing two Greek words together (*anti* – against, and *nomos* – law). This refers to those who preach that the Old Testament Scriptures are useless and have no redemptive value for the post-ascension believer in Jesus. (This in spite of the fact that the moral law of God as found in the 10 Commandments were cited constantly in various phrases in the New Testament epistles as well as the Gospels.)

We see a revival of this today in the hyper-grace teachers and pastors who say we don't actually need to follow the teachings of Jesus in the Gospels. Moreover, in an attempt to appeal to the culture, there have been some sloppy sermonic attempts to "unhitch the Old Testament from their faith."[304]

Whether intentional or not, this kind of teaching can lead to a falsely dualistic view of the Bible, in which the Old Testament God is a vengeful Judge and the New Testament God is a God of love. However, He remains the same loving God throughout all time—even when He brings judgment, it is motivated by love.[305] We also see through the frequent citation of the Old Testament in the Gospels and the epistles that the Old Testament informs our faith and is just as crucial to our faith as the type, shadow, and foundation of the New Testament.

2. Gnosticism

Gnosticism is a form of teaching developed by the heretic Marcion of Sinope. Essentially, this was a derivative from Platonic teaching, which stressed that the spiritual world was more important than the natural, fleshly, material world—which resulted in a dualistic view of reality and core values.

Preachers and church movements today who only focus on escaping the earth and going to heaven teach a form of semi-Gnosticism. Teachers who

---

304   Andy Stanley, "Aftermath, Part 3: Not Difficult // Andy Stanley," YouTube video, 39:44, April 30, 2018, https://www.youtube.com/watch?v=pShxFTNRCWI.

305   Heb. 13:8

stress only the spiritual life, individual salvation, and prayer—to the exclusion of living out the reign of Christ practically on the earth and influencing culture—are practicing dualists who get their cue from an unbiblical Gnostic heresy, even if they are true believers in Jesus. The apostle John stresses the facts of Christ's incarnation and His creation of the material world to combat this false teaching.[306]

3. Pneumatomachianism

Pneumatomachianism, also called Macedonianism, is a fourth-century Christian heresy that denied the full personality and divinity of the Holy Spirit. According to this heresy, the Holy Spirit was created by the Son and was thus subordinate to the Father and the Son. Those who accepted the heresy were called pneumatomachians, or "spirit fighters."

In orthodox Christian theology, God is one in essence, but has three personas—Father, Son, and Holy Spirit, who are distinct and equal. Present-day Jehovah's Witnesses and Mormons teach that the Holy Spirit is an impersonal force. Surprisingly, a poll taken by the Barna Group illustrated that a large percentage of Christians also believe the Holy Spirit is only a symbol, but not a living entity.[307]

Although I don't hear any evangelical or charismatic teachers preach this heresy explicitly, I have noticed that many believers treat the Holy Spirit merely as a force or power from God. Instead of understanding that the Holy Spirit is someone we are called to fellowship with as the third person of the Trinity, many people seem to think the Holy Spirit was sent to merely energize, anoint, or heal them.[308] To ignore the divine personhood of the Holy Spirit is to ignore a key part of God's essence.

4. Arianism

Arianism is the idea that Jesus is a creation of God, as He is God's Son, thus demoting Christ from His fully divine nature.[309] It gets its name from

306   John 1:3, 14; 1 John 1:1-5, 4:1-3

307   The Barna Group, "Most American Christians Do Not Believe That Satan or the Holy Spirit Exist," April 13, 2009, https://www.barna.com/research/most-american-christians-do-not-believe-that-satan-or-the-holy-spirit-exist/.

308   2 Cor. 13:14

309   Encyclopedia Britannica, s.v. "Arianism," last modified July 23, 2019, https://www.

the fourth-century priest Arius, who first posited this idea.[310] The Council of Nicea in 325 A.D. combatted this heresy and created the Nicene Creed in response.[311]

Arianism's popularity spread despite its denouncement and continues to spread today. A present-day revival of this old heresy of Arianism has re-emerged through the popularization of writings and teachings of 19th-century teacher Charles Taze Russel, who also denied the Trinity, taught pneumatomachianism, and preached that Jesus was Michael the Archangel. His teachings now claim about 20 million adherents in the movement known as Jehovah's Witnesses.

Church, we need to be grounded in the way of Jesus and His apostles. Delve into the Word and soak in what the Lord has to say, then live out what He tells you. Let us not be led astray by the teachings of this world. May every reader diligently search the Scriptures; connect to a Jesus-honoring, biblical church; and earnestly desire to know God so they can make Him known. Amen.

---

britannica.com/topic/Arianism.

310   Ibid.

311   Ibid.

THE NEED FOR A GENERIC PROPHETIC STANDARD IN THE BODY OF CHRIST

The following is the backdrop for a "Prophetic Standards Statement" that Dr. Michael Brown and I initiated with input from dozens of prominent national charismatic leaders in the spring of 2021. Dr Brown wrote an article on it that has the following explanation.

In the lead-up to the 2020 elections, Bishop Joseph Mattera and I began to discuss the need to convene a number of charismatic leaders, sensing the fallout that would come should Trump not win reelection.

The first conference call took place on February 8, with about twenty leaders participating, and without names being released. That led to the drafting of a Prophetic Standards document, which was then submitted for discussion during a second call on March 15, involving most of the same leaders and some others who had not been part of the first call.

During that second call, the document was reviewed line by line, resulting in many changes and improvements. Then, it was sent to a number of other key charismatic leaders who were not part of either call, resulting in further sharpening of the statement.

It is, therefore, a group statement rather than that of any individual or denomination or stream or network or group.

As for the initial signers, they, too, represent different denominations, streams, networks, and groups, including megachurch pastors, biblical scholars, theologians, evangelists, leaders of apostolic networks, recognized prophetic ministers and local church leaders.

It is our hope that this statement will both honor and encourage prophetic ministry while at the same time calling for greater accountability, since unaccountable prophecy has been a bane on the modern Pentecostal-charismatic movement for decades.[312]

312   Michael Brown, "Kingdom Leaders Make Unified Call for Prophetic Accountability," April 29, 2021, https://www.charismanews.com/opinion/in-the-line-of-fire/85262-kingdom-leaders-make-unified-call-for-prophetic-accountability.

PROPHETIC STANDARDS STATEMENT

At a time when there are many questions in the Body concerning the gift of prophecy and the ministry of the prophet, and in light of the needs of local pastors as well as individual believers to have practical guidelines for processing prophetic words, as Pentecostal and Charismatic leaders, we felt that now was the opportune time to produce this current document.

It is not the purpose of this document to condemn or accuse. Instead, our purpose is to help provide Scriptural guidelines for the operation of the gift of prophecy and the functioning of the ministry of the prophet, while at the same time affirming the importance of these gifts and ministries.

We believe that the gifts of the Holy Spirit, including the gift of prophecy and the ministry of the prophet, are essential for the edification of the Body of Christ and the work of the ministry, which is why Scripture exhorts us to earnestly desire spiritual gifts, especially that we may prophesy (see 1 Cor. 14:1, 39). Prophetic ministry is of great importance to the Church and must be encouraged, welcomed, and nurtured.

We believe it is essential to create an environment in which prophecy can flourish side by side with the other gifts of the Spirit and together with apostolic, evangelistic, pastoral, and teaching ministries. To create this environment, we need to encourage freedom in the Spirit in a faith-filled atmosphere, making room for spontaneous utterances as the Spirit wills. But all this must be done with proper accountability and oversight.

We believe that the general function of the gift of prophecy, as it relates to the church, has to do with edification, exhortation, and comfort (see 1

Cor. 14:3). As this gift relates to unbelievers, it can reveal the secrets of their hearts and bring them to repentance, demonstrating God's reality to them (see 1 Cor. 14:24-25).

We believe that the essence of the spirit of prophecy is the testimony of Jesus. Hence the ultimate goal of prophetic ministry is to exalt the lordship of Jesus Christ, even though we recognize that not every prophetic word will specifically point to Him (see Rev. 19:10; 1 Cor. 12:3).

We believe in the five-fold ministry of the prophet, recognizing that such prophets will also be used to bring correction, instruction, and directional clarity to the Body, but not independent of other leaders, and therefore different from the model of the independent Old Testament prophet.

We recognize that prophets do not serve as spiritual fortune tellers or prognosticators, nor is their role to satisfy our curiosity about the future or reveal abstract information. God's purpose in prophecy is redemptive, calling for repentance, giving supernatural guidance, bringing comfort, deliverance, and restoration, and glorifying Jesus as Lord.

We recognize that, due to the nature of prophetic ministry, some prophetic words can be submitted for evaluation before they are delivered while other words will be evaluated after they are delivered. But in all situations, those claiming to speak for God should welcome the godly evaluation of their prophecies. Those who refuse to have their words tested should not be given a platform.

We believe that prophecies should first be tested by the Word, then if the prophetic word is not contrary to the Scriptures, it should be evaluated by other mature leaders. If a prophecy is given in the context of a local church, then mature leaders in that setting should evaluate it. If a prophecy is given in the context of a region or nation, then mature regional or national leaders should be invited to evaluate the word (see 1 Cor. 14:29; 1 Thess. 5:19-21).

We recognize that prophets receive supernatural revelation from God, but they are also dependent on other five-fold ministry leaders for the interpretation and application of the revelations they receive. It is the Lord's will that all these various ministry gifts, including the ministry of the prophet, work in harmony rather than independently. Only then will the Body come into full health and maturity.

We recognize the unique challenges posed by the internet and social media, as anyone claiming to be a prophet can release a word to the general public without any accountability or even responsibility. While it is not possible to stop the flood of such words online, we urge all believers to check the lives and fruit of those they follow online and also see if they are part of a local church body and have true accountability for their public ministries and personal lives. We also urge prophetic ministers posting unfiltered and untested words from the Lord to first submit those words to peer leaders for evaluation.

We agree that the Scripture instructs us not to despise prophecies but to examine prophetic utterances carefully and to hold fast to that which is good (see 1 Thess. 5:19-21). This also means that we should cultivate honor and respect for true prophetic ministries rather than an attitude of skepticism or scorn.

We believe that all spiritual leaders, including those serving as prophetic ministers, should be vetted and qualified by their respective churches, networks, or movements based on the standards of leadership set forth by Paul the apostle as found in 1 Timothy 3:1-8; Titus 1:5-9.

We believe that all spiritual leaders, including five-fold ministry prophets, should be above reproach and should live a life worthy of their calling (see Eph. 4:1-3). Consequently, we believe that prophetic leaders whose lives violate the moral and ethical standards of the Word disqualify themselves from the ministry irrespective of how much influence or anointing they have.

We also agree that the greatest requirement for all leaders in the church, including prophetic leaders, is to endeavor to reflect the character of Christ and to utilize their gifts out of love for God, His people, and the lost (see 1 Cor. 13:2; Rom. 8:29).

We value humility, integrity, and accuracy in prophetic ministry in order to protect the faith and trust of those who hear a word that is stated to be from God. It is a sacred thing to claim to speak for the Lord and, in keeping with the words of Jesus, to whom much is given, much is required (see Luke 12:48). And just as those who teach are held to a higher standard of accountability (see Jam. 3:1), so also those who prophesy should be held to a higher standard. They can have a powerful influence over people's lives for better or worse, because of which we urge sobriety and circumspection together with faith and boldness.

We understand that prophecies can be conditional and that many prophecies will take time to come to pass. We also recognize that prophetic language is often mysterious and symbolic, requiring interpretation and insight. This means that prophecies that do not contradict the Bible or that are not contrary to fact should be evaluated over time and not immediately rejected.

On the other hand, if a prophetic word is delivered containing specific details and dates in which the stated prophetic word will come to pass and that prophecy contains no conditions to be met in order to be fulfilled, and that word does not come to pass as prophesied, the one who delivered the word must be willing to take full responsibility, demonstrating genuine contrition before God and people. Any statement of apology should be delivered to the audience to whom the erroneous word was given. For example, if it was given to an individual, the apology (and/or explanation/clarification) should be delivered to the individual. However, if the word was delivered publicly, then a public apology (and/or explanation/clarification) should be presented. This is not meant to be a punishment, but rather a mature act of love to protect the honor of the Lord, the integrity of prophetic ministry, and the faith of those to whom the word was given.

We believe it is essential that all spiritual leaders, including prophetic leaders, have a presbytery of peers and seasoned spiritual leaders who can hold them accountable regarding their life and ministry. In keeping with this, we reject the notion that to judge a prophet's words is a violation of Psalm 105:15, where God exhorted the ancient nations not to touch the patriarchs or harm his prophets. Prophets who err must be willing to receive correction from peer leaders with whom they are in accountable relationship. Those refusing such accountability should not be welcomed for ministry.

We recognize that true prophetic words can be faith-building and can sometimes call for a faith-filled response, but we reject the idea that prophets can use Old Testament texts about believing the prophets in order to gain blanket support for their words, as if everything a prophet utters today must be believed. To the contrary, we can only believe the prophetic word if it is not contrary to Scripture, it is not factually in error, and our own spirits bear witness with it. Only then can we add our faith to that word coming to pass (see 1 Tim. 1:18).

Those wanting to use Old Testament prophetic texts to exercise influence or authority over their followers should remember that inaccurate prophecy under that same Old Testament standard was punishable by death. New Testament prophets, along with other New Testament ministry leaders, do not lord it over their people or demand submission and faith. Instead, in humility, they serve the flock (see 1 Pet. 5:1-4).

We reject any threatening words from prophets today, warning their followers that judgment will fall on them if they fail to obey the prophet's words. We see this as a dangerous form of spiritual manipulation.

We reject the spiritual manipulation of the prophetic gift for the personal benefit of the prophet or his ministry, whether to garner favor, power, or financial gain. And under no circumstances can a prophet charge money to deliver a prophetic word. This is spiritual abuse of the worst kind and is detestable in God's sight.

We reject the notion that a contemporary prophetic word is on the same level of inspiration or authority as Scripture or that God always speaks inerrantly through prophets today, since the Bible says we only know in part and prophesy in part (see 1 Cor. 13:9). It is the written Word alone that can lay claim to being "the Word of God" (see 2 Tim. 3:16); prophecies, at best, are "a word from the Lord," to be tested by the Word of God.

Finally, while we believe in holding prophets accountable for their words, in accordance with the Scriptures, we do not believe that a sincere prophet who delivers an inaccurate message is therefore a false prophet. Instead, as Jesus explained, and as the Old Testament emphasized, false prophets are wolves in sheep's clothing, in contrast to true believers who might speak inaccurately (see Matt. 7:15-20; Jer. 23:9-40; Ezek. 13:23). Thus, a false prophet is someone who operates under a false spirit masquerading as the Holy Spirit.

We therefore recognize distinctions between a believer who gives an inaccurate prophecy (in which case they should acknowledge their error), a believer who consistently prophesies inaccurately (in which case we recognize that this person is not a prophet and we urge them to stop prophesying), and a false prophet (whom we recognize as a false believer, a lost soul, calling them to repent and be saved). Because God's gifts and calling are irrevocable (see Rom. 11:29), we understand that a person who has been prophetically gifted might be able to function in that gifting even though they are no longer in right relationship with God. That is why it is imperative that we judge a prophet by the fruit of their life and ministry rather than by their gift, also recognizing that there are some who started right but will be rejected in the end (see Matt. 7:21-23).

Original Signers
Aaron J. Robinson (MDiv. PhD candidate)
Alan Hirsch (100 Movements)
Apostle John Kelly (International Convener for ICAL)
Archbishop William Mikler (Communio Christiana)
Barbara Wentroble
Bishop Dale Bronner (Theology doctorate)
Bishop Joseph Adefarasin (Guiding Light Assembly, Lagos, Nigeria)
Bishop Joseph Mattera (Dmin. THD)
Bishop Julia Whitehurst Wade (founder of Perfecting Covenant Prevailing Connection)
Bishop Kyle Searcy (DTh., Fresh Anointing Church)
Bishop Reford Mott: (MDiv. DMin., Generations Church, New Rochelle NY)

Bishop Richard Callahan (D.Min. D.D. President of Maranatha Ministerial Fellowship, Intl.)

Bishop Tommy Reid (Niagara Pastors Fellowship)

Chris EW Green, (PhD)

Chris Palmer, (MTS and PhD candidate)

David Balestri ("Executive Consultant" of Elite Human Development," Australia)

Dennis Peacoke (Go Strategic and The Statesmen Project)

Doug Stringer (Somebody Cares CEO)

Dr. Al Warner (Set Free Inc. Executive Director, DMin.)

Dr. Cheryl Bridges Johns (PhD)

Dr. Craig Keener (PhD)

Dr. Dan Hammer (founder Son Rise Christian Church, Dmin)

Dr. Daniel Juster (THD, Tikkum Ministries Israel)

Dr. Doug Beacham, (D.Min., General Superintendent and Presiding Bishop, International Pentecostal Holiness Church)

Dr. Edgar González (J.D., D.Min. Global Impact Ministries, President)

Dr. Greg Williamson (Valley Christian Center)

Dr. Israel Pena (PhD, Leader of "The FLOW Kingdom Ministries")

Dr. Larry Stockstill, (D.D., Director of Pastors University)

Dr. Mark Chironna (Dmin. PhD candidate)

Dr. Mark Kauffman (International Network of Kingdom Leaders)

Dr. Mark T Barclay (Rev., MB, PhD, Mark Barclay Ministries)

Dr. Marsha Wood (MACE D Min. MA. Overseer of His Tapestry International Ministries)

Dr. Michael Brown (PhD)

Dr. Paul VanValin, (PhD, founder Eden Counseling and Consulting)

Dr. R. Heard (founder of numerous international schools)

Dr. Randy Clark (D., D.Min., Th.D., M.Div., B.S. Religious Studies, Overseer of the Apostolic Network of Global Awakening, President of Global Awakening Theological Seminary)

Dr. Roberto Miranda (President of New England Alliance; Congregación León de Judá/Congregation Lion of Judah, D.D., PhD)

Dr. Ronald V. Burgio (D Min, Vice President Elim Fellowship)

Dr. Sam Storms (PhD)

Dr. S.Y. Govender (MD., ABC Ministries, South Africa)

Dr. Wayne Grudem (Ph.D. Distinguished Research Professor of Theology and Biblical Studies)

Evangelist Daniel Kolenda (President and CEO of Christ for All Nations)

Fred Markert (founder of The Great Awakening Project)

George Runyan (City Church Ministries)

Giselle Bonilla (Prophetic GPS)

Jennifer LeClaire (founder of Awakening House of Prayer)

Jeremiah Johnson

John Burton (popular author, Bible teacher, revivalist)

Joshua Kennedy

Jonathan Tremaine Thomas (President, Civil Righteousness, Inc.)

Ken Fish (Dmin. candidate, founder of Orbis Ministries)

Kris Vallotton

Loren Sandford

Mark Aarstad (MDiv. PHD candidate)

Mark Driscoll (Founding Senior Pastor, The Trinity Church and Real Faith Ministry)

Michael Wells (Apostolic Leader of C.A.M Leadership Network)

Negiel Bigpond (Two Rivers Native American Training Center President and founder)

Niko Peele (Ignite Movement Network)

Pastor Bojan Jancic

Pastor Charles Flowers (Sr. Pastor, Faith Outreach, International CEO of San Antonio in Black, White and Brown)

Pastor Darrian Summerville (City Servants Church)

Pastor Don Nordin (CT Church, Houston, Texas)

Pastor Joel Stockstill, (Director, Surge Project)

Pastor Les Bowling

Pastor Marc Estes (Senior Pastor of Mannahouse, President of Portland Bible College)

Pastor Mark Pfeifer (Open Door Church and Soma Family of Ministries)

Pastor Mike Servello (Compassion Coalition founder and CEO, Redeemer Church, Utica, New York)

Pastor Richy Clark, (Freedom Church, Magnolia, Texas)

Pastor Steve Riggle (MA. DMin, Founding Pastor of Grace Church, President of Grace International Churches and Ministries)

Pastor Vince Thomas, Jr. (M.A. The Outlet Community Church, Atlanta, Georgia)
R.T. Kendall (D.Phil)
Robert Gay
Ron Cantor
Steve Trullinger (PhD, The Father's Touch Ministries)
Steven Strang (CEO of Charisma Media)
Thamo Naidoo (International leader of The Global Gate Family, South Africa)
Tony Fitzgerald (Church of the Nations)
Ward Simpson, (CEO of God TV)
Will Ford (Director of the Marketplace Leadership Major at Christ For the Nations Institute)

To view an up to date list of all the signers, to sign the document, or to download it, please go to https://propheticstandards.com/.

RECOMMENDED READING

Healing and Christianity: A Classic Study by Morton T. Kelsey. This is a comprehensive history of healing in the Christian Church from biblical times to the present.

The Kingdom and the Power: Are Healing and the Spiritual Gifts Used by Jesus and the Early Church Meant for the Church Today? edited by Gary S. Greig and Kevin N. Springer. Celebrated Reformed theologians, including J.I. Packer, Wayne Grudem, Stanley Burgess, and Jeffrey Niehaus, examine the validity of arguments against miraculous and revelatory gifts in the Church today.

ABOUT THE AUTHOR

Dr. Joseph Mattera is an internationally known author, consultant, and scholar whose mission is to influence leaders who influence nations. He leads several organizations including The United States Coalition of Apostolic Leaders. He has a DMin. from Bakke University, THD from Antioch University, and is a PhD candidate.

instagram.com/josephmattera

facebook.com/josephmattera

twitter.com/JosephMattera

Joseph Mattera

OTHER BOOKS BY DR. JOSEPH MATTERA

The Jesus Principles

Walk in Generational Blessings

La Bendicion Generacional

Poisonous Power

Understanding the Wineskin of the Kingdom

25 Truths You Never Heard in Church

The Divided Gospel

Cutting Edge Leadership

An Anthology of Essays on Apostolic Leadership

Ruling in the Gates

Travail to Prevail

Kingdom Revolution

Kingdom Awakening

To order his bestselling books or to join the many thousands who subscribe to his acclaimed newsletter, go to www.josephmattera.org.

eGenCo

Generation Culture Transformation
Specializing in publishing for generation culture change

Visit us Online at:
www.egen.co

Email us at:
info@egen.co

facebook.com/egenbooks

youtube.com/egenpub

pinterest.com/eGenDMP

instagram.com/egen.co